MIRACULOUS POWER OF THE SUBCONSCIOUS MIND

MIRACULOUS POWER OF THE SUBCONSCIOUS MIND

(Ultimate Guide to Health, Wealth and Enlightenment)

Dr. N.K. Sharma

PRABHAT PRAKASHAN

No part of this publication can be reproduced, stored in a retrieval system or transmitted in any form or by any means, electronic, mechanical, photocopying, recording or otherwise, without the prior permission of the author and the publisher.

Published by
PRABHAT PRAKASHAN PVT. LTD.
4/19 Asaf Ali Road,
New Delhi-110 002 (INDIA)
e-mail: prabhatbooks@gmail.com

ISBN 978-93-5186-712-8
MIRACULOUS POWER OF THE SUBCONSCIOUS MIND
by Dr. N.K. Sharma

© Reserved

Translated by
Ashutosh Garg

Edition
2025

Price
₹ 400.00 (Rupees Four Hundred only)

Printed at
Shree Sai Printers, Sahibabad

Dedication

To all the people and youth of the world
who, by realizing the infinite powers hidden within
can touch the ultimate heights of prosperity,
can fulfil all their dreams and desires,
can change the scenario of the entire world,
can create a unabridged prosperous,
healthy and blissful society!

"The Whole World, Its People and even animals all are purely governed by their subconscious mind. Wherever we are! Whatever we are! We are absolutely by-product of our subconscious mind. If you want to understand yourself and the whole humanity (The ultimate truth) you have to learn and understand about subconscious mind."

—Dr. N.K. Sharma

Preface

The whole of humanity is governed and ruled by our subconscious mind. All our behavior, personalities, habits, reactions, traditional followings, customs, achievements, success and failures are a result of our own beliefs and conditioning. Remaining unaware of this greatest gift of nature which we are born with is just like not using the hi-tech machinery you bought for your factory just because you don't know how to use it.

It's a matter of great concern that the magnum human power which governs the whole humanity every moment, 24 hours a day even in our dreams (i.e. sleep), and still it is not a part of the curriculum in our education system. In our day to day life, we hear about it a lot, we often talk about it, we come across this word many a times in our normal routine, but we have never been taught this subject in schools. Though a small portion of this vast topic is taught to students who pursue Psychiatry but very few psychiatrists really know about this subject in detail; because if they would have seriously studied and understood about the subconscious mind they could have become truly spiritual and an awakened soul. They themselves would have enjoyed the benefits of it in their practical life as they wished. But unfortunately I found very few psychiatrists with a truly balanced life. Ironically many of them are troubled with their own problems. Reading a subject and **'living'** a subject (here it is the subconscious mind) are altogether an entirely different aspect.

Even in this modern advanced scientific era no steps have been taken to teach this subject in schools or colleges. Because of this lack of a proper medium to impart knowledge about this subject to the general masses, other alternative institutions are mushrooming to cater to the needs of those who are truly interested in the subject. People interested in these subjects try and learn it through hypnosis, NLP, Secrets of law of attraction, Creative Visualization, Mind Power and Subconscious Mind Programming workshops. But that is not even one percent of the world's population.

Is it not a irony that 99% of the world's population has never learnt or heard about this greatest gift of nature – The diamond, which they possess throughout their life and die without even knowing and using its miraculous powers.

This book is a small effort to enlighten the masses of their unique power. The more one knows and explores his mind powers specially the conscious and subconscious mind, the more he moves towards a path of enlightenment. The super consciousness also known as Awakening, Sakshi Bhav, The observer, Vigilant Soul .Presently we are the slaves of these two minds, the moment you understand the original functions of these two minds it then becomes **YOUR** choice how to use it. You can master your whole personality, your behaviors, your future, your destiny, your desires and dreams. You can choose hell or heaven. You can rewrite everything. An Enlightened soul has no mind; they use their mind when they need. Mind is for unawakened people who work without their permission, therefore so much illusions, so much blind belief, so much confusion. Even our ego is nothing but our subconscious image which we develop over a period of time without our knowledge and we succumb to it for our whole life. Our God, our destiny, our circumstances, our future, our achievements, our relationship, our health, wealth, youth and happiness – we attract everything and create according to our beliefs. By understanding your subconscious mind, you will understand the whole humanity in total and above all your own self.

This book indeed is extraordinary in its presentation as I have covered all those subjects which you will not generally find in any book on subconscious mind written so far. I have tried to expose and shatter all our common blind beliefs, illusions and fears which we face in our day to day life such as wish fulfillment, flashes of your religious Gods, our religious rituals, ghost illusions, varieties of destinies, our poverty and richness, early aging and youthful long life, your unexplainable dreams, unexpected human behavior, our natural psychic powers (intuition, telepathy, etc.) our success and failures etc., so many invisible mystic phenomena which are nothing but purely a reflection of our subconscious powers or beliefs.

When we do not understand how and why it all happens; God, priest, astrologers, black magician, psychic expert come in between and we surrender ourselves completely to their advice and suggestions just because of our sheer ignorance of the powers of subconscious mind.

This book will definitely help a common man to come out of his ignorance and master his mind as he desires.

—Dr. N.K. Sharma

Contents

1

Miraculous Power of the Subconscious Mind

Man is the most amazing creation of the Universe upon whom God has bestowed all His powers before sending him down on this Earth. The creator has filled such wonderful powers in His son that the latter is capable of creating absolutely anything by using them. Today, after gazing on the man's development in recent years where man has converted impossible into possible, Almighty must also be wondering that how is own creation has surpassed his own creator. God provided the raw material but man converted into wonderful articles. He gave rocks, man turned them into temples; God offered wild forests; man converted into beautiful gardens. God provided only mineral one and man-extracted metals and built utensils, aeroplanes and jewellery.

Man is Next to God

We are the source of the ultimate creation in this Universe. Whatever we dream of and think about, sooner or later, manifests itself and the element that plays the pivotal role in these manifestations is – our conscious mind and subconscious mind. Conscious mind is the master, while the subconscious is the slave. Whatever thoughts and desires the conscious mind create, the subconscious mind immediately readies itself to fulfil those thoughts and desires. The subconscious does not argue or resist as it does not possess a mind of its own. The power to resist and argue rests only with the king, the conscious mind. The subconscious mind, like an obedient army, simply follows the commands given by its king. The king can only make plans, but the execution and success of the plan is the duty of the army. The subconscious mind has the power of the commandos which are always ready to lay their lives for the sake of their master. In the process, the king prepares his army to follow the instructions, but gradually the army assumes such enormous authority that it starts governing the king. After a certain point of time, the king becomes so

helpless at the hands of his own army that it is the king only who, by his sense of awareness, needs to revert the process and keep its army from going astray. It simply implies that the weaker the king (conscious mind) becomes, the army (subconscious mind) keeps getting stronger in the same proportion. However, it is also true that the army does not differentiate between the good and the bad and it merely follows the commands of the king.

The conscious mind through its argumentative power fills the subconscious mind with good and bad thoughts and the subconscious then becomes responsible for fulfilling those good and bad deeds. Let us now try to understand the concept of the conscious and the subconscious mind.

□

2

The Conscious Mind and the Subconscious Mind

The human mind is divided mainly into two parts – the outer (conscious) mind and the inner (subconscious) mind. The conscious mind analyses, thinks and gathers all kinds of information. However, the subconscious mind is the subtle mind where all the memories – those of the childhood, of the present life remain etched. It converts the repeatedly given instructions into habits. The subconscious mind accepts the slightest signal given to it by the conscious mind and starts working to materialize the signal. An indication (habitual thoughts), provided by the conscious mind is received instantly by the recorder of the subconscious mind. We are hardly aware of such a phenomenon taking place and it is only later on that we realize about the kind of instruction that we have provided to the subconscious mind.

The conscious mind is the external manager whereas the subconscious mind is the internal manager. After we sleep, all the regular functions of the body are carried out with precision and perfection such as beating of the heart, digestion, hormonal balance, maintaining the blood chemistry and reacting aptly to the right and wrong food combinations. By communicating a thought to the subconscious mind through our conscious mind, we can restore or disturb the balance of various chemicals and hormones in our body.

Conscious mind has limitations while the subconscious mind is limitless. The conscious mind can work only on the physical world and physical body level while the subconscious can travel anywhere in the astral world. It is beyond time and space and is capable of travelling in the past and future. It can communicate with anyone anytime within a fraction of a second. The subconscious mind is known to resonate our desires, feelings and thoughts and attract similarly related waves to fulfil those desires and thoughts in the Universe.

Our subconscious mind is the most powerful transmitter in this Universe. The television, radio, satellites and even the most efficient of wireless systems have their limitations but the subconscious mind can transmit our thoughts and feelings to anywhere in the Universe. That explains why Telepathy (distant transmission of thoughts), is so easily possible!

Our subconscious mind can reach out to anyone in this Universe and search the hidden secrets, see them directly and explain them to us accurately. The subconscious mind is the receiver of the source behind the power of intuition amongst humans. By making the conscious mind calm and quiet, we can easily see, hear and feel the events of the past, present and future through intuition using the power of the subconscious mind.

Professional astrologers, tarot card readers and crystal ball gazers use these powers of the subconscious mind to earn name and fame. It is a myth amongst the laymen that such powers are possessed only by a chosen few – the siddhas (the enlightened). But the fact is these natural and divine powers are present in every person by birth and can be realized and acquired by everyone with a little practice. People often experience these powers unknowingly, but they tend to disregard them considering these experiences as mere coincidences. Each one of us get fleeting glimpses of the unlimited powers in the form of intuition. It only proves that by understanding the working and science of the subconscious mind, we can, if not completely, utilize it partially and transform our lives as per our wish.

It is amazing to note that 90% of the human brain is under the control of the subconscious mind and it is only the remaining 10% that is under the control of the conscious mind. It only proves the point that the conscious mind has very less role to play in our life, while the subconscious mind enjoys unlimited powers. Most of out time of the day is governed (as per the programming done by our old habits), by the subconscious mind. The conscious mind is used only when we have to learn a new practice or acquire a new habit. The conscious mind acquires its knowledge by using the library of five senses organs (eyes, nose, ears, tongue and touch). The information gathered by these senses organs is used by the conscious mind to formulate opinions and arguments. Owing to this, the conscious mind stops working after a point of time and its limitation comes to the fore. Poets, writers, artists, scientists and everyone else know that when the conscious mind stops working, it is the subconscious mind that responds and gives solutions to life's everyday problems. Your powerful desires make the subconscious mind work and materialize your desires from the unlimited wealth of the Universe. This is often referred to as the divine guidance.

All great inventions and discoveries of the world are the result of an intense desire and passion for a particular thing exhibiting the mammoth power of the subconscious mind. The conscious mind can only produce trivial things. It is a known fact that whenever the conscious mind gives up in despair its pursuit of a question, it is the subconscious mind which comes out with an answer from its unlimited reservoir of knowledge. The answer was available even earlier while one was busy finding it with the help of the conscious mind. However, the tension and stress was not letting one see it. Once the mind becomes serene and calm, the solution emerges from the subconscious mind.

Whatever feelings are subdued by us, accumulate inside us. These come out as soon as the conscious mind becomes inactive. That is why a drunkard, in the state intoxication, speaks the truth though incoherently, which he cannot speak otherwise. The same principle is used in Narco Test on criminals in which, they are injected with benumbing drugs as it causes them to lose control over their conscious and thus, the truth comes out through the subconscious mind.

We often express our inner feelings while sleeping as the conscious mind is inactive during that time. Negative state of mind and in acute depression too, the conscious mind loses control. Thus, a person is likely to speak his heart out in such situations. Anger is also a similar state wherein a person expresses his real feelings. While in the conscious state, a person is able to subdue his thoughts and feelings and can tell a lie easily. In this context, I have written a few lines:

Feat of Anger

Never abandon anger from your life,
It has achieved great feats in this world out.

Man usually speaks the truth when angry,
while angry words from heart sprout,
He weighs the pros and cons of the past,
as it helps to realize his potential very fast,

Everyone's face in anger reveals his mind.
But anger unveils the reality behind.
Anger can distinguish kind from a cruel,
It is not the man, but ego that boils.

□

Every Person has a Dual Personality

What we see is not our real personality. Our real self is revealed when we face an emergency, problem or in a moment of crisis or opposition. At such time, we do what our subconscious mind directs us to do.

Wherever there are two personalities, tension prevails. The real personality is not required to be covered; it is quite natural. It is only the unreal self which needs to be taken care of as the false aspects of our personality tend to get uncovered often.

Meditation shatters the barrier between the conscious mind and the subconscious mind and develops the feeling of witnessing life. An unconscious mind or a worldly person is governed by two minds whereas a meditative person becomes free from the duality of the conscious mind and the subconscious mind. He does not have any past or future. He dictates his mind as per his own will. He lives in both minds alike and wanders freely from one mind to the other.

When the feeling of observance intensifies with meditation, the conscious mind fails to develop. The more intense the unconsciousness becomes, the deeper the subconscious mind delves. The entire existence of the subconscious mind depends on the information furnished by, the directions given by and the dreams seen by the conscious mind. Unless the conscious mind transfers all these things to the subconscious mind, the latter cannot grow because the subconscious mind is the slave to the conscious mind. We may say that the activity level of the conscious mind is directly proportional to that of the subconscious mind. The more active is the conscious mind, the more active the subconscious mind becomes. During meditation, as the conscious mind become calm, the subconscious mind also becomes serene and quiet and all its dreams disappear. One is not likely to dream while meditating because in the state of observance, the activities of the subconscious mind are not active. Awareness breaks the boundary wall of the subconscious mind. This state is referred to as enlightenment and *moksha* (salvation). One who is devoid of the subconscious mind becomes the Buddha, the enlightened.

□

Two Major Principles of the Subconscious Mind

1. Any thought, action or feeling when repeated becomes a part of your inner self.

It is called programming or conditioning. It is the outcome of repeating a habit. It is a fact that no habit – good or bad – develops on its own; it is acquired with practice.

2. The subconscious mind cannot differentiate between reality and imagination.

It behaves alike in both the situations because while speaking truth and also while imagining, we create a specific type of thought pattern and feelings. In both the situations, the subconscious mind exhibits certain reactions as it doesn't differentiate between the two. As the conscious mind develops a strong faith through imagination and visualization, the subconscious mind reacts accordingly.

As per the first principle, at the time of our birth, our brain is just like an empty cassette (though the *sanskaras* of the previous birth are fully present in your subconscious mind), and thereafter, we are made to practice all the activities. We are taught how to eat, how to eat and drink, how to bathe, how to behave, etc. A work that is repeated

by us 8-10 times becomes a part of inner self and then it manifests in our behaviour in the form of habit. Thus, we become an effigy of hundreds of habits. Contrary to this, a person living alone in the wild hardly develops a few habits.

When we initially learn to drive a car, scooter or a bicycle, we remain completely conscious and focused. However, after regular practice, driving becomes a part of our inner self and then we are able to drive a vehicle even without consciously focusing on it. It is a very amazing example of how less we use our conscious mind while practicing such habits. The conscious mind comes into action only when a new activity or a habit is learned.

Likewise, we can discuss several other similar habits. Women, hardly concentrate while making *chapattis* or cooking routine stuff in the kitchen. Their mind wanders elsewhere and still they are able to do their work efficiently. When we brush out teeth or take bath, our hands and other body parts move exactly the same way everyday. All our actions and behaviour during the 24 hours become our habit and that is why we can call ourselves an effigy of habits.

While talking, we often tend to add phrases like 'I mean', 'actually', 'really' etc. to maintain the flow of our talks. However, gradually we notice that the use of these phrases and terms forms a part of our habit and we cannot talk without using these expressions even when they are not required.

□

Mind is not Restless; We Practice Restlessness

It is usually said that mind is very active. However, it is a myth. Mind is not at all active and the entire process of making it active or hyperactive is a thoroughly practiced phenomenon. The more information the mind receives, the more active it becomes. Sometimes, we ourselves contribute in making the mind overactive. Instead of focusing on one work at one time, we try to indulge in multi-tasking. We don't even enjoy a cup of tea properly as we hardly remember taking 5-7 sips from the cup; during the rest of the sips, our mind keeps wandering here and there in London, Mumbai, office, business, news, TV, etc. We ourselves make the mind hyperactive by not focusing on a single

activity. We become what we practice. Consequently, when we want to focus on something, the mind habitually wanders elsewhere and it becomes almost impossible for us to control it and concentrate. It only proves that if we can practice multi-tasking, we can also practice concentration. The only difference between you and Lord Buddha is that He fully lived in the present moment. If He would drink tea, he would have all the 25 sips of his cup of tea, He'd walk with complete focus while taking a walk. He is able to do it because that is what He practiced and what He practiced He became! We consider it to be miracle or His greatness. You must also practice to concentrate and do not try to use your sense organs for different types of activities. While listening to music, you should try to enjoy only the music. While talking on phone, focus only on the conversation on phone. Just bathe while bathe, just eat while you eat. Likewise, learn to focus on a single activity at a time; it will gradually become your habit and you will begin to feel like the Buddha. Whatever activities we see and hear from our childhood, those become a part of our lifestyles.

These are the direct *samskaras* which you acquire through repetition. There is another category of indirect samskaras which become a part of our innerself without our knowledge. Despite the subconscious mind disliking these habits, they get passed on to the subconscious mind and form our habits. Simply imagine that you are extremely soft-spoken and peace-loving person and abusive language is not at all used in your house and family. However, owing to a fight amongst the neighbours, you are forced to listen to their abusive language. Now, whenever next time, if you get into a quarrel with someone, those abusive terms, will naturally and unintentionally come out of your mouth.

Long back, there was temple near our house and I could hear the chanting of the mantras early morning. I used to get disturbed by those sounds as I would be still asleep at that time. However, today after a span of 50 years, even if recite one line of one of those mantras, the entire mantra comes back to my memory though I never really tried to memorize them consciously. Likewise, anything that passes through our sense organs repeatedly, becomes apart of our innerself. Thus, we fill our minds with numerous things unknowingly. This also explains why we reflect many of the behaviour and thoughts of our teachers, parents and relatives who remain close to us for longer periods.

The herd mentality also has a similar effect on us. If your subconscious mind is not strong enough, you will tend to become a part of the crowd. If you see everyone clapping, you also begin to clap and afterwards, you ask as to what is the matter. If the crowd is running, you also start running with them without knowing the reason. While with the crowd, you are controlled with the crowd's mind and not your own mind. With regular meditation, awareness and a feeling of observance, you can break this tendency.

A 2-3 years-old child neither goes to school nor anyone teaches him to talk, but the child by merely listening to your everyday conversation learns your language and starts speaking it clearly and fluently. This is Indirect Programming. All advertisements on TV and radio carry out indirect programming. When you see or listen to an advertisement again and again, it leaves a mark on your mind and you start humming with it. Hoardings also leave an impact on the subconscious mind. We are simply the reservoir of innumerable information gathered through our various sense organs.

Subconscious Mind Does not Differentiate Between Reality and Imagination

As soon as we imagine something consciously, be it negative or positive, our subconscious mind catches those vibrations and begins to react. Accordingly, our body chemistry and hormones start working. Our entire body chemistry and hormonal system is under the control of the autonomic nervous system which in turn is governed by the subconscious mind. This implies that through our imagination and visualization, we can instantly control our hormones, blood chemistry, autonomic nervous system and the subconscious mind in a positive or negative way.

We are aware of the fact that whenever we imagine something soothing, our body feels relaxed and light whereas it immediately begins to feel restless and tensed at the thought of a negative emotion. It indicates that an ordinary thought – real or imaginary – can instantly affect our body functions and their working.

A casual imagination has a mild impact whereas if the imagination is coupled with positive or negative emotions, the impact increases greatly. Our beliefs and fears deeply influence our mind and body. It depends on how seriously or casually the emotion is felt. To understand this, let us take an example. Consider a person standing atop a 20-storey building and looking beneath. Till he is enjoying looking at things down under, he feels happy and thrilled, but as soon as the dreadful thought of falling over the building crosses his mind, he feels a shiver running down his spine. The man has not fallen down but merely the thought of it happening disturbs him and causes perspiration and anxiety. Such positive or negative imaginations can refresh or ruin our lives. You can now imagine as to how many such worthless thoughts lead to constant disturbance in our body and hormones throughout the day.

More Examples to Understand the Effects of Thoughts

Suppose you had a quarrel with someone and owing to the insult undergone at the hands of the other person, you get angry, your BP shoots up, your fists get tightened and you become breathless. Thereafter, the incident ends and you go back to your house. While returning, if you again think about the incident and the insult, all reactions – anger, rising of the blood pressure, fists getting tightened and breathlessness – surface again. Now, you are not actually having a fight but the thought process inside your subconscious mind triggers the same hormonal and bodily reactions you had experienced earlier at the time of the actual incident.

The best example is that of tamarind. You must have surely tasted tamarind, unripe mango or lemon. The taste any of these watered your mouth and send a mild shiver down the spine. Now, if you merely see someone having any of these sour eatables, your mouth fills with water and in some cases, the shiver is also felt. Therefore, you just imagined the sour taste but your subconscious mind treated it to be real and made the body react in a manner that it feels real.

If you simply imagine that you are roaming in an orchard of lemon trees and there are lemons trees all around. Then you plucked a lemon from a tree, cut it with a knife and squeeze the entire lemon juice inside your mouth. On opening your eyes you will find that your mouth is filled with water. In fact, while imagining the whole scene right now while reading this article, you may have a watery feeling in your mouth. This is the amazing impact of imagination on the subconscious mind.

Suppose you go to a friend's house as a guest and the host serves you bowl of extremely delicious *kheer*. The *kheer* was so tasty that you go on praising the *kheer*. Suddenly, a small child of your host friend comes and tells you that their pet dog had unfortunately, licked that bowl. Now, despite the fact that you were all praises for the *kheer*, suddenly on hearing about the dog licking the bowl, you feel nauseated and restless. And then again the child tells you that it was the other bowl which the dog had licked and your bowl was clean, you feel at ease and relieved.

It is a fact that even if an incident does not take place actually in our life, we create an upheaval in our hormones and blood chemistry merely imagining it. This causes health or disease depending on our thought pattern. The intensity of our visualization determines its impact on our body system. Ramakrishna Paramhansa was a famous saint of Bengal. While starting the *sakhi* sect in the worship of Lord Krishna, he imagined himself to be a woman. His imagination was so intense and powerful that he developed breasts like women just in 3 months. Moreover, his gait and voice also turned feminine. It is also mentioned in this context that when his feminine visualization intensified further, he even started to have menses after 6 months! This is the miraculous and incredible effect of indomitable faith!

As a token of reverence towards the God, various types of miracles such as walking on fire, piercing needles in the body, lying on bed of thorns, taking out *pooris* with bare hands from boiling oil are nothing, but live examples of the commands given to the subconscious mind. In a Rajasthani village named, 'Badi Sadri', of the Chittorgarh area, all ladies of the village have to prove their fidelity and purity by taking out ten *pooris* each with bare hands from the vessels containing boiling oil. It is surprising that all the ladies accomplish this feat easily because their subconscious mind feels that since they are loyal and pure their hands will not get burnt. This powerful and emotional thought is accepted by the subconscious mind and it gets materialized.

It is the Imagination that Makes or Mars

It is indeed very surprising whether or not an event is actually taking place. Human being begins to imagine it happening, thereby leading the subconscious mind to make positive or negative changes in the hormones and chemicals of the body. It is even more surprising

that mostly such imaginative feelings are negative and full of fear and apprehensions. If a child is not told stories about ghosts and spirits in his childhood, he will never feel afraid of such things in the dark. Since he has listened to such tries and concepts, he creates these apparitions in his imagination and start believing in them.

If an astrologer tells you that you are going to die after a week, your subconscious mind begins to imagine the death. Now irrespective of the fact whether death actually takes place or not after 7 days, but the effect of its imagination on the subconscious mind will surely cause loss of appetite, you face will become pale and you will start losing weight.

A religious Hindu person who worships his Gods in various forms (Hanuman, Durga, Shiva or Krishna), imagines the presence of these Gods with such intense emotions that these Gods even appear in his dreams. If you are devoted towards some Guru, you will begin to feel your Guru's presence everywhere around you and you may even talk to him. The fact actually is that our subconscious mind makes us see whatever we wish to see with powerful emotions. However, a Muslim or a Christian will never report to have seen any of the Hindu Gods. They will only see their own Gods whom they worship. The Chinese will see a God with a long beard while, a Japanese will see a God that looks more like the Japanese. Likewise, there are thousands of examples. We are the by-products of the conditioning of whatever we have heard and have been

taught since our childhood. The only thing that can break this conditioning is meditation, awareness and observance.

Man is not lustful by nature, but as soon he sees a woman and imagines about lustful actions, the body instantly gets heated up and the body organs become excited. At times, this excitement reaches its peak and a man may even experience discharge of semen. It is the best example of the powerful impact of imagination on the subconscious mind.

While watching an emotional film or a scene, we often feel like crying. When our conscious mind reminds us that we are sitting amongst several people in a theatre, we tend to control our feelings and do not express them openly in public, but if we are watching the scene alone, we are sure to cry. The incidents are happening in the film, but we imagine them to be place in front of us which causes our subconscious mind to treat it as real and thus it prepares the body to respond accordingly. If you do not imagine irrelevant incidents and events, the subconscious mind will remain dormant thus having no reaction on the body. And it is only through meditation that we can break the chain of imagination and thoughts.

Our conscious mind is like a lens of the camera and the subconscious mind is like the film. The conscious mind selects the scenes based on its belief and logic and the subconscious mind simply accepts and prints them. Conscious mind is the gardener that waters and nourishes whatever seed – be it *neem* or mango or poison – is sowed in it by the conscious mind. Therefore, subconscious mind is only the servant of the conscious mind. It is so loyal that it never refuses to obey your command and fulfills all imaginations of the conscious mind with utmost devotion. Its main duty is to follow the instructions – positive and negative – of the conscious mind.

If you say that your memory is poor, your subconscious mind immediately responds and says, 'Yes Master, your memory is poor' and if you say your memory is very good and that you remember everything, the subconscious mind repeats that, 'Yes Master, your memory is very good'. If think that a work is tough to be accomplished, the subconscious mind accepts it and if you think a work to be easy, that is also accepted by the subconscious mind. You can say that the voice of the subconscious mind is the echo of your conscious mind. Whatever you speak or think will come back to you.

Since childhood, our parents, friends, relatives and teachers give to us various kinds of concepts and thoughts. To these, we also add some of our thoughts with age and experience. This is how our psychology of positive or negative thoughts is created. This psychology in turns determines the success or failures in our life. For those who often face problems and failures in life, should learn to become aware early. Those who already have success and prosperity can rise even higher.

Subconscious mind is your *jinn*, your *kaamdhenu* (a cow that fulfills all desires), your *kalpvriksh* (a tree that fulfills all desires). It provides you whatever you desire from life – good or bad – anything you wish for!

It is strange but true that poverty and prosperity are not bestowed upon people by God. They are our own choices. The rich and the poor have entirely different thought pattern is in their lives. A poor man always thinks that he has to keep working for money and that he does not have money and this becomes true – he is always short of money! The rich, on the other hand, has the reverse. He thinks that money works for him and that he has enough money to fulfill his dreams and desires. That is also true – he always has ample money to spend!

The poor man says – "This is beyond my reach". This thought itself closes the doors of receptiveness and the subconscious mind fails to accomplish anything for him. Whereas, the rich man says – "I will create it with my

efforts." His subconscious mind senses the receptivity and instantly responds and starts working to fulfil his desire. Therefore, both poverty and prosperity are the results of our own thoughts. Those, who detest money and see it as a source of sin, remain poor or middle-class as they program their minds to merely work for salary, pension, security, etc. and they tend to remain dependent on others for their success. Thus their subconscious mind limits them within fixed boundaries.

A rich man always lives outside the comfort zone. He keeps thinking innovative and constructive things. He feels confident with his self-esteem and indomitable spirit. He programs his subconscious mind to achieve and accomplish anything in life and his subconscious mind, in turn, materializes his desires.

Dreams and thoughts may be unrealistic, but no dream or no thought is unadvisable for the subconscious mind. Those who reach the pinnacles of success in their lives have had dreamed to be at that pinnacle thousands of times earlier, and one fine day, their subconscious mind makes their dream come true. Nothing is impossible for the subconscious mind. You are free to dream and imagine; it is the duty of your subconscious mind to realize your dreams and imaginations. It is man who limits himself and remains pegged to the mundane wants of life. Those who dream big, achieve big. The intensity of our desire and imagination determines the time that is taken to achieve the desire.

Man's dreams to fly in the sky and go to the moon are fine examples of the power of the subconscious mind. Today, all these dreams have been fulfilled. It is also a fact that in future, whatever man dreams to achieve will surely get realized with his fervent desire and aspiration by the power of his subconscious mind. You will appreciate that at an earlier point of time, when seeing dreams was prohibited and there was not much scope of imagination, the development of society remained slow. However, ever since man learned to dreams and aspire, the progress made in various aspects of life has been astounding. Numerous discoveries, inventions and the development made by man is the result of our dreams, desires and imagination. It is the display of our amazing psychic and human powers. Therefore, one should not undermine the value of imagination because it is this imagination – positive or negative – that fulfills our desires.

Imagination plays a crucial role in our lives. Our present life may be smooth, but as soon as we imagine about a specific kind of a lifestyle, our present life seems to become unbearable for us. We instantly wish to have the imagined type of lifestyle. Though, in reality, there has been no change in our lives and the change has taken place only at the imaginary level but we become restless and sad. Thus, it becomes clear that our life is mostly based on imagination and less on reality.

Suppose we get to hear the news of the death of some relative. Though we have not actually seen the person in the mortal state, but we start imagining all sorts of things and the subconscious mind brings about changes in our mood and behaviour. However, if someone tells us that the news was incorrect and the person is alive and fine, our pattern of thoughts immediately change and we feel relieved and happy. The subconscious mind again makes instant changes and our mood and behaviour begins to alter accordingly. Here, the point to be understood is that neither of the event has actually occurred in front of our eyes; it is only our imagination that affects the subconscious mind which in turn affects our mood and behaviour.

Deep conviction and blind faith makes the subconscious mind achieve even the most improbable tasks such as walking barefoot on fire, piercing sticks through body, sleeping no the bad of nails, etc. They are able to tolerate the severest pain, keep prolonged fasts, walk excessively long distances, climb high peaks and bathe in chilled water and ladies burn with the pyre of their husbands. Sometimes, this is also used to catch thieves. It is pronounced that one who is a thief, eats grains of raw rice, will begin to bleed in the mouth. This imagination brings necessary changes inside the body chemistry of the real thief and when he is made to eat rice, bleeding in his mouth occurs. Therefore, it is the imagination of our conscious mind which is blindly accepted by our subconscious mind which in turn brings the required changes in our body.

Often girls think and behave like boys; this brings changes in their hormones and other body organs and in due course of tie, they tend to become masculine. By repeatedly thinking about pain, loss, grief, we can easily induce diseases like diabetes, blood pressure, cancer etc. It needs to be understood clearly that the incidents causing tension are only temporary and last for a short period of time, but by retaining them in our memory for longer periods and repeating them through words and thoughts, we increase the effect of such incidents upto 100 times and harm ourselves immensely.

□

No Mantra Works Without the Help of the Subconscious Mind

The entire success of a mantra depends on the subconscious mind. All mantras – of any language – work only by the power of subconscious mind. Language affects only the conscious mind. It is actually the feeling (intention) deep-seated inside our subconscious mind that works! The vibration produced by the mantra is actually of our intention that affects the subconscious mind. There is no power in the word or the language of the mantra. The power resides in the intention with which the mantra is chanted. That explains as to why mantras of all languages tend to work successfully and bring about the desired effects. If you consider the word *'laddoo'* (a kind of round sweet) equal to God, and start chanting, *'laddoo laddoo...'*, it will produce the same effect as the word, 'raam raam..' or 'allah allah...' provided your intention should be that *'laddoo'* is your God and it will surely fulfil your desire. This is the

reason why different names of different religions are easily accepted and they also work successfully.

If you believe in a God or chant a mantra only at the conscious level, it does not have any effect on the subconscious mind. All forms of worship, *siddhis* (achievements) and success are due to the subconscious mind. These are often named as the blessings of God. It is a fact that God is hardly interested in your success or failure. He has provided you with all the requisite means to make your life blissful. It is your choice to make or mar your life. The world is governed by the indisputable Laws of Nature. God has framed these Laws long back. Now He has no role to play. One who understands and adheres to these Laws wins and succeeds in life, while the one who ignores and refutes them loses in the game of life! In fact, the Universe is not governed by God, but by the rules made by God. Had the will of God prevailed, there would not have been differences of caste, creed, poor and rich, success and failure, etc. These concepts have been created by man, not by God. If we are able to comprehend the powers of the subconscious mind and the laws of Nature, we can easily get rid of human-induced concepts.

□

7

Subconscious Mind – The Creator of Our Destiny

Amusingly, God is simply not interested in framing or deciding our destiny. It is we who knowingly or unknowingly attract good or bad destiny for ourselves. Whatever thoughts and emotions we create through our conscious mind using our logical brain, those are recorded around our soul in the form of *samskaras*. That is what makes our subconscious mind. Soul is just the carrier of our good and bad *samskaras* and the soul is not affected by the fact whether our *samskaras* are good or bad. Those persons who have dissolved their good and bad *samskaras* are known to become Buddha and Mahavir. When we go into the state of trance, the conscious mind loses its grip and we can clearly see the events of our past lives which are recorded in the subconscious mind. I have proved this fact by taking thousands of

people in their past lives and making them see the events of their past lives.

Destiny is the outcome of all that we have earned through our good and bad deeds in the past. Future destiny is dependent on our deeds that we are going to do henceforth. So simply by becoming aware and by changing our deeds consciously, we can improve the present and hence the future. Whatever we do today frames our future. Therefore, future is clearly in our own hands and God has no control over it. Enlightened persons like Buddha and Mahavir succeed in dissolving their future completely as they lose the feeling of being the doer of their actions.

□

8

We Attract Coincidences and Soul

There is nothing as coincidence in this Universe. Neither is God interested in creating any such coincidences. Whatever impression – good or bad – we leave on the subconscious mind through our actions create happy or sad effects in our lives which we tend to call coincidences. Our deeds – good and bad – makes a mark on the subconscious mind and that in turn brings good and bad situations or persons in our lives. These decisions are not taken by God. Our entire life is the result of the impressions on the subconscious mind. That is why knowledge of spirituality is required here. By understanding and adhering to the Laws of the Nature and leading our lives on complete awareness, we can attract any person, situation, emotion etc. in our life.

It is important to understand that no purpose is served by taking God's name, trying to please Him by various means, remaining afraid of Him, or by wasting money in the name of worship. Instead of utilizing their money on the development of society and mankind, people prefer spending huge amounts of money in the name of God. It is not wise to sit idle and think that whatever God wills will only happen, so why should we work. The above mentioned concepts are hardly related to spirituality. In fact, they merely symbolize the blind faith, fraud and ignorance being followed in the name of religion and spirituality. All these are nothing but spiritual follies of people living in utter ignorance.

The various forms of Gods and Goddesses that we believe in, are merely the figments of imagination created by our subconscious mind. Meditation and awareness release us from the bondage of these figments. If a saint or a sage or hermit is still tied to the worldly affairs and pays more attention to his clothes, long braided hair, beard, *tilak* (mark on the forehead), spiritual ornaments, crystals, smearing of ash etc., it only means that he has not yet been able to comprehend the secrets of the subconscious mind. The one, who realizes the futility of the above symbols and becomes free from the bondage of these, is wise.

□

9

All Tantra, Mantra and Yantra are Gimmicks of the Subconscious Mind

No tantra, mantra or yantra has the power of its own. We create a belief system with our thoughts and convictions and after accepting them, when we use the tantra, mantra and yantra. They seem to produce the desired effect. Every religion has its own tantra, mantra and yantra. Which one will you believe? The most interesting thing is that all these tantra, mantra and yantra are man-made and each person can charge these objects with specific intention. The power of our emotions and intentions can charge any object powerfully. It needs to be understood that the power does not reside in the object or an idol of God, or an amulet. When you treat these objects with respect and reverence, these get charged with the power of your feelings and intentions and give you the desired result.

It may be appreciated that the religious books and

scriptures kept in the bookshops are simple books printed alike on the paper but it is your reverence and regard for these books that make you realize the divine feeling in them. Any object, if seen with reverence, generates the divine feeling of God in it. And the object, in which the divine feeling is generated, becomes powerful.

While using a charm or an amulet, there is a feeling of security and success attached to it. This creates a positive and a deep sense of feeling which in turn affects the subconscious mind. The more it affects the subconscious mind, the more are the chances of success. It is not the yantras and amulets that cause an event to take place, but the positive imagination which is then accepted by the subconscious mind. Once accepted firmly by the subconscious mind, it begins to realize the desired imagination. It is, therefore, clear that the success and failure of yantras, tantras and mantras depend on nothing but solely on the power of your intention and visualization.

□

Imagination can Transform Your Life and Future

Through the power of our imagination, we can easily transform our habits, nature, personality and quality of life as per our will. What we are today is the result of the programming of our subconscious mind since past several lives. Likewise, our future will be framed the way we programme ourselves today. When we record a song on a blank CD, the same song keeps playing until we record another song over it. You must remember that the tape-recorder does not record the song on its own; it records what we want it to record. We also know that when we record a new song, the earlier song is erased automatically. Similarly, we can erase the previous programming done in the subconscious mind and re-programme the subconscious mind to achieve new aims and objectives.

We can put new habits and qualities in our personality, accomplish impossible tasks, reverse the ageing process to remain young forever, become millionaires, create so many things, get charged with immense energy, live blissfully always, develop awareness in our life, become Buddha, fill our lives with love and remain unperturbed with joys and sorrows of life. All this is possible within a period of 30 days!

Owing to the ignorance about the powers of the subconscious mind, the saints sages and hermits in the past have been trying, though unsuccessfully to conquer the mind. Today, the various types of worships and practices have been developed only to fight against the subconscious mind and gain supremacy over it. On seeing the possibly impossible tasks, accomplished by the subconscious mind, the sages and saints used to call it miracle or God's grace. However, the powers of the subconscious mind have today been discovered and become known to us and we now realize that we can achieve anything and everything in our life using these miraculous powers.

Earlier we used to think that Gods has been kind to us and that is why we have been able to achieve a particular aim, but actually it is the subconscious mind that enables us to do it. You may worship Shiva, Durga, Hanuman, Ram, Kali or any other God but the result is always given by the subconscious mind. The supreme power that works for us is actually our belief and faith in the God and it is irrespective of the type of God that you worship. This is the reason why amulets and charms of all religions and beliefs seem to work successfully.

God is not an entity. The cosmic energy spread in this entire Universe and which is governed by the indisputable Laws of the Nature is what we term as God. The Universe is nothing but the collection of a large number of energies. As the man creates the seeds of feelings and desires and conjoins them with the emotions of the soul, the only thing that gets affected and influenced by the vibrations of these intentions is our subconscious mind. And as soon as the subconscious mind is affected by these vibrations, it sends them in the Universe and begins to attract the related energies from the Universe. It is a Law of the Nature that like energies attract each other. It is very important for us to understand that nobody in this Universe is concerned with you. It is our wish either to create dreams and desires, and throw the vibrations in the Universe or to sit at home and remain satisfied with what we have. We are actually the creators of new things in this Universe. Your desires and thoughts are the seeds; God simply provides nourishment for the growth and development of these seed. There was a time when man had limited dreams and limited desires and that was the reason why he could not get enough from the Universe. However, it is not so today. As the dreams and desires of man are increasing steadily, his creations and achievements are also on the rise in the same proportion. If the same zeal continues, time is not far when man will be able to fulfil all his dreams successfully. This Universe is the reservoir of unlimited knowledge and powers; we must increase our own ability to receive from the Universe. I have tried to express this fact in my way –

"Humse zyada ishwar ne hamara kiya vichaar hai
Khoob lutaane baitha wo, loot lo, jo taiyaar hai."

(The God has been kind enough to think about us more than we do; He is ready to give generously, one who is ready, can receive it).

The only agent, representative or the entity responsible to receive the gifts of the Universe is our subconscious mind. Unless you can send extremely powerful and focused vibrations of your dreams and thoughts into the Universe using your subconscious mind, no result can be achieved. As a result, in the absence of a clear and powerful signal from the subconscious mind, the Universe will not be able to provide you the desired things. Therefore, it is essential to learn the art of influencing the subconscious mind in a powerful and effective manner.

□

Your Future is the Result of Your Present

There is no independent existence of Future. The future is the creation of our present. The seeds sown in the present determine the yield of the future. The subconscious mind is not affected by the quality and taste of the seeds; it does not matter if the seeds are of positive or negative thoughts. The subconscious mind is only responsible for nourishing the seed. Our everyday thoughts, actions, emotions directly or indirectly affect the subconscious

mind which in turn accepts these thoughts and creates our future by attracting similar vibrations from the Universe. A person living in complete awareness sows the seeds of his thoughts and acts carefully, thereby creating the future of his choice. **Future is a concept only for the unaware people; those who are aware do not have any future as they live only in the present moment.** For such a person, concepts like past and future become meaningless. Therefore, unless man learns to become aware and appreciate the difference between the conscious and the subconscious mind, all his religious acts and spiritual endeavours are worthless. The gist of all spiritual exercises lies in becoming aware and uniting with the Truth. Therefore, those who wish to frame their future as per their wishes should immediately abandon anger, irritation, criticism, hatred, fear etc. and sow the seeds of happiness, love, affection, compassion, prayer. If are able to do this well, our future will be just like we want it to be. There is no power in this Universe that can stop the future from being so.

It is important to watch yourself throughout the day to see whether or not you are putting the seeds of positive or negative thoughts in your subconscious mind. Sowing the seeds of happiness means that all your day whatever work you do – drinking, eating, prayer, singing, office work, house work, etc. – should be done gladly. Works done with annoyance, anger and disinterest leads to negative thoughts being sown. Therefore, if the present is full of happiness and heavenly then our future also becomes happy. The concept of going to heaven after death is incorrect. Heaven is a misconceived notion for the people who are ignorant, unaware and enjoy living in illusions. The real heaven lies in being aware and conscious. The only way to make your present enjoyable is to do everything joyously, happily and with gratitude. If you succeed in living the life this way, you will be full of bliss otherwise you will lose this opportunity. It is your life and your time; you are free to make your life the way you wish it to be. If you miss the chance, nobody except you will be affected. Therefore, it is your wish to become aware or to remain ignorant, but the subconscious mind will continue to give positive and negative results depending on our thoughts.

□

12

God's Glimpse is a Gimmick of Subconscious Mind

World-over all the saints and sages such as, Meera, Chaitanya, Ramkrishna Paramhansa, etc. whose fables about realization of the God are available in the religious and holy scriptures. Even today we hear that people who are devoted towards their Gods and Goddesses talk to their Gods and are even guided by them, saved from accidents and negative energies. But is it really true? If yes, is there any science that works behind all this? Let us try and understand it.

Every religion preaches two forms of the God – the formed and the formless. Both are based on faith and belief. The kind of faith will determine the kind of image that will be formed in the mind. If the mind worships Durga, Hanuman, Ganesh or Shiva and keeps thinking about them. This causes the conscious mind to gather the vibrations of these Gods and builds a matching aura. Therefore, whenever you close your eyes and dream, you tend to see the images of the God that you have been thinking about and whom you worship all day. The intensity of thought determines the clarity of the image. The more intense and powerful the thought, the better and clearer image is formed. Since it is just like a wish-born child, produced by your own thoughts, it appears to you like a Godly form. This further increases your faith. If you are a Hindu, you will always see Hindu Gods and Goddesses, Muslims will see Mecca-Medina or some other Sufi saint, Christians will tend to see Jesus, Chinese monk will see God with a moustache and beard.

The above instances prove that the story and the faith which is put forth before you in your early childhood and repeated before you for the rest of your life becomes a part of your innerself. However, it is dependent on your belief and acceptance. A Hindu may have seen the images of other Gods also, he may also have been to a Mosque or a Church or a Gurudwara but, deep inside his self, he lacks the acceptance for these Gods and hence the subconscious mind does not get affected by the Gods other than those of his own religion. Inside a Church, a Hindu may bow his head down but it is not due to reverence for Jesus, but only to hide his embarrassment in front of the others. Likewise, Muslims and Christians also do not get affected by the Hindu Gods and Goddesses. That is why our saints have well said – **"jaki rahi bhawna jaisi, prabhu moorat dekhi tin taisi"** (In whatever form one visualizes God, one experiences Him in that form).

By repeatedly thinking and visualizing about something

creates a powerful aura around your being and this powerful aura is called 'spirit'. This spirit will come before you each time, you think about it. It will guide you, talk to you and protect you. Depending upon your wish, it will change its form and keep working for you. Just as there is no real existence of ego, but it develops gradually due to your belief and imagination about yourself, the Gods and Goddesses also leave a trail on your being. It is a human nature to consider ego and image as real. Actually there is no existence of ego. If you ask yourself – where is my ego and image? The reply you get is – inside my being. And the being resides in the imagination; it does not exist in reality. A few people talk about you, praise you and you tend to immediately decorate those comments and remarks in your being, in your imagination. Ego can develop only with the existence of other people; there can be no ego in solitude as you do not get praise and comments in solitude. Meditation and awareness can shatter the ego because meditation does not permit irrelevant imaginations to take place.

If you are not shown any image or told nay story of any God in your childhood, the fact is that you will have no concept of the existence of God and there will be no programming of Godly feelings in your subconscious mind. It is only after you imagine about God that the subconscious mind can accept the notion.

It is not that man believes in God because he loves God or that he likes the concept of God; man believes in God because he is afraid of death, diseases, destiny, planets and that he has problems, desires and dreams. So basically, man is not a God-loving creature, but a God-fearing creature. And he continues to live in this illusion all his life. If man would not have problems and desires, he would have never believed the existence of God. A verse says it all:

Maut ne kar diya laachar varna
insaan vah khudbeen hai ki

khuda ka bhi kaayal na hota

(Had it not been the fear of death
Man is such an egoist creature that
he would never believe in God)

Therefore, all human efforts and endeavours to praise God and please Him are based upon the fear that God is such a powerful entity which if not praised and pleased will bring havoc upon man and if praised and feared will save man from all dangers and problems. Man also wants a place in heaven, which he thinks is possible only by chanting God's name. However, these are all myths which are propounded in all religions and man follows them blindly. Owing to this false notion, our entire energy, wealth and all efforts are being diverted to praise the Almighty instead of being spent on scientific development and research. I have put it in my own way –

Sadiyon se log na jane kyu parmatma ko rijha rahe hain
Khokar apna amulya samay khud ko thaga rahe hain
Parmatma koi vyakti nahi jise khushamad ka intezar hai
Vah to prakriti ka niyam hai,
jispar chalna hi saccha aachaar hai

(Why, ever since, people are trying to please God why do
they waste their time by duping themselves God is not a
human being, waiting to be praised He is Nature's law,
pursuing which is the real cure).

The other form of the God is the formless one wherein the believers assume that God has no definite form. However, this notion is also given to us for the first time and gradually repeating this concept gives rise to various types of imaginations. It changes our perspective and then the concepts of various forms and shapes of Gods and

Goddesses do not affect our minds. It is an altogether different kind of programming of the subconscious mind. It is also an illusion and man continues to live in this illusion throughout his life. Such illusions and blind beliefs have led to hatred and wars in the world. It is amazing that there is no concept of God in Jainism and Buddhism because belief or disbelief in God does not lead to any basic change in humans. As per these two religions, the word 'God', has not originated due to any desire to see Him or to attain knowledge, but due to the desire to get rid of pain and suffering. This is the reason why both these religions prohibit idol worship and religious rituals. However, it is also a fact that despite these prohibitions mostly there are Jain and Buddha temples. The reason behind this is the fear and helplessness of man. It is human nature to find a support system to lean on and a form or a shape fulfills this human need. It is not incorrect to say that Gods and Goddesses are pegs fixed on the walls of life and man has been clinging to these pegs for support. But it must be remembered that the pegs do not support you; it is the conviction and belief with which you cling to these pegs that supports you. Therefore, it does not matter whether the peg to which you are clinging is of Hanuman or Durga or Sai Baba; what matters is that faith with which you are holding on to the peg. This strong conviction and belief can make you perform any impossible task, be it climbing a mountain, walking on fire or observing a stringent fast.

There are thousands of such pegs in this world and innumerable persons are clinging on to these pegs. It makes their life easy. It is a kind of mental conditioning which is quite necessary for an ignorant person otherwise he is called an atheist. An Atheist does not believe in God and hence feels miserable in moments of pain and suffering because his ego and fanatic notions do not permit him to bow before the Almighty. There is no substantial difference between an atheist and a theist. Both are tied to their own individual

beliefs and live in different kinds of illusions.

One who is an enlightened person is fully aware that the whole world, including man, is nothing but God. But our ego (image) does not let us see the Truth. It is to be noted that by having notions of a particular God, a specific religion, a caste-creed, a particular dress or by having a specific image, man will never be able to understand God though he lives in the illusion of believing in God. How can a person tied to a particular mental conditioning experience God? Once these curtains of delusions disappear, man becomes truly religious and a real *yogi*.

□

Eternal Youth or Early Old Age is a Gift of Subconscious Mind

It is surprising that youth or old age of our body is determined by our subconscious mind which receives and accepts the kind of thoughts we transfer to it. Truly speaking, old age comes at a very later stage in our life when we cross the age of 80 years. However, if we want we can feel like a young man even at that age and perform all youthful tasks with ease like, rock climbing, horse riding, swimming, running, playing games, going to the gymnasium and doing everything without getting tired or exhausted.

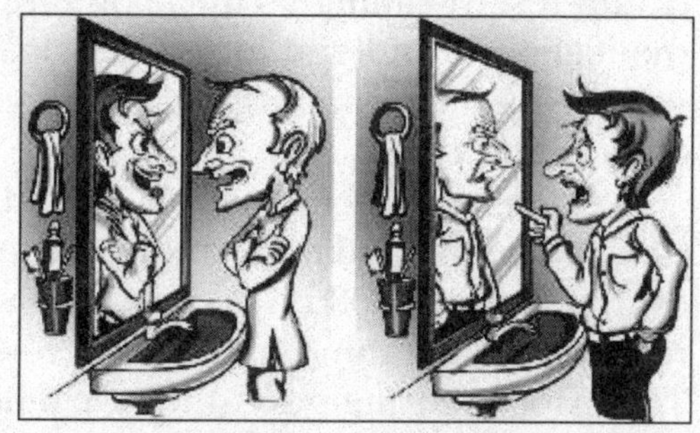

There is huge difference in the old age of the Western and the Eastern countries. In the Western countries, there are no servants to help and mostly people till the age of 70-80 or even 90 have to work on their own. Therefore they tend to become self-dependent. On the contrary, in the Eastern countries such as India, old people are taken care of by their servants, children and daughter-in-laws etc. so they become dependent on others. That is why people become lethargic and start looking old at the age of 50 years.

In India, old age is the result of the conditioning of the subconscious mind and the unnatural lifestyle. A person nearing 40 starts using spectacles begins to lose teeth one after the other and his hair turn grey. Repetitive statements about getting old create a lasting impression on the subconscious mind. As a result, by the age of 40-45, a person suffers from some or other disease. At the turn of 50, sugar, blood pressure, heart problem, joints pain and exhaustion begin to seep in. It has become our mindset to treat these problems as a part of our age and essential problems of the old age!

Our mind is conditioned to believe that by the age of 50 years, we are bound to have some or the other disease because it is a conventional thing to happen. Then we get ourselves medically insured. After our kids grow up and children start calling us uncle or aunty, it further enhances the feeling of old age in us. This leads to a constant and permanent programming of the subconscious mind to accept old age and diseases.

After retirement, people in India are referred to as 'senior citizens' and their children also do not let them work on the pretext of their old age. This leads to an adverse reaction on the mind and it suppresses their zest for life. They stop wearing good-fitting clothes and begin to wear loose and dull clothes. Their choice of music changes and they start listening to religious songs and music. Spiritual bend of mind and visits to temples and places of pilgrimage creates an impression that one is getting old. One starts thinking that about death and begins to take God's name and chant mantras. Acts such as reading scriptures and chanting God's name are harbingers of old age.

As our age advances, our interest in life's activities reduces and we treat every work as worthless. We think that we have eaten enough, drunk enough and made enough merry. As soon as we retire we stop learning and creating new things. The fact is that any age, at which we stop learning and creating, is the end of our life. It shows we have become stagnant like a water pond which is devoid of any fresh water. Such a person, under the garb of social and financial security, is merely passing his time aimlessly. There are countless such young people who are old by heart; most of them are in India and the majority are in the government sector!

Old people do not listen to new songs, watch new films, read new books, appreciate new art forms and relish new programmes because they are pre-occupied with the memories of the past. An old man always lives in his past. He measures everything of his present and future with his past. We must remember that the country or the society or its citizens who merely keep alive their past memories and pay less attention to the new experiments and discoveries, can never develop and progress.

Life is all about the present moment. There is nothing in the past or the future. Change is an inevitable part of life. We all know that everything changes with time and it is an ongoing and continuous process. The country or the civilization that remains attached only to its past and fails to take the change in its stride will lag behind the rest of the world.

Memories of the past mean old age! The present reality and the dreams for the future indicate youth! Therefore, one who keeps learning, creates new things, makes new plans, sees new dreams and works unrelentingly for the realization of those dreams remain young and youthful even at the age of 100 years. Time may bring about changes in the physical body but the real matter – the mind – lies within, and that needs to remain young! A brand new car with an old driver cannot run fast, but if the driver is young, he will steer away even an old car swiftly!

Youth Means a Zealous and Creative Life

It is the duty of man to live zealously and creatively till the last breath of his life. It is the real secret of youth. Wear good clothes, be smart and take full interest in all activities of life – art, music, science, literature, sports, social service etc. Always keep your mind open and receptive to learn and experience new things. Even at the age of 90, one must plan new projects and work on them. Never think – I have done enough, what new remains to be seen or done – as it only means that you have stopped flowing with the present moment and have become stagnant in the past. You must realize that whatever you have lived, eaten and seen was in the past. The past is now over. It is dead. Life is ever blooming with new buds, new flowers, new music, new creations, new hopes and new dreams. If you go on looking at the past, you will miss the blissful moments of the present life – the real life.

Wearing white or saffron clothes in the name of spirituality is a sham, a deception. Get out of it. Those who are unable to transform from within, for them changing from outside is meaningless. Enjoying the pleasures of life is not wrong but the feeling of attachment with them or creating fear or ego out of these things is wrong. Live and enjoy, forget the past and be ready for the future. This is what I say –

kal ka sukh fir chahiye, aisi koi chaah nahi
aaj mila vah dhanya hai, dil ko ab parvaah nahi

(There is no desire to experience the pleasures of the past
I am happy with what I have today, it makes me carefree).

Therefore, treat this temple of body with great care and love; ornate it the way you decorate the idols of God. Perhaps you believe that there is no God within you, that is why you enjoy living a simple life.

log na jane kyun khuda ko bahar dhundhte hain
shayad unhe yakin hai ki unme khuda nahi

(It is inexplicable why do people search God outside
Perhaps they are sure that He does not live in them)

Listening to new spiritual stories every other day is like watching a mountain from a distance. Merely to chant God's name make idealistic statement is not '*satsang*'. The real meaning of '*satsang*' is to live with the virtuous, the truth and the positive. It is like living with the Nature. Plants, animals, music, literature, art, people, meditation, prayer, jokes, happiness, sports, socializing, creativity, science, inventions and discoveries, and the entire cosmos is the source of '*satsang*'. Living harmoniously with the creations of the Nature is also *satsang*. Considering *Satsang* to be merely chanting the name of God is a sign of a constricted perspective. Music that stirs your soul is Godly, like the songs sung by Mohd. Rafi and Lata Mangeshkar, give you a glimpse of God. You cannot ignore those songs by saying that they are filmy or romantic songs. Love is the highest form of spirituality. If you can see the glimpse of God in the various forms of art, there could be nothing bigger in life.

The real meaning of spirituality consists in absolute liveliness, pleasure and blissful expressions. Gloominess, dullness, stubbornness, stringent lifestyle, a specific way of dressing, baldness, etc. all are enemies of happiness and contrary to spirituality. They signify mental illnesses and a faulty conditioning of the mind. It is necessary to safeguard ourselves from these diseases.

In order to remain youthful, to look bright faced, to remain active and agile, you will have to make believe your subconscious mind through imagination and belief system that you want to work and remain active that you want to learn and do new things. If you succeed in creating a picture in the subconscious mind of your wish to remain agile, active and that of taking interest in all the activities, your subconscious mind will do the necessary spadework to make this all come true for you.

However, for this to happen, you should have your own image of a 25 year-old boy. Even if it is imaginary, it is essential to make you feel active, agile and youthful. Your ways of working, sitting, standing and walking should be those of a 25 year-old boy, only then your subconscious mind will believe it to be true and then it will create the necessary hormonal changes inside your body so that it will give a youthful look to your body, face and personality. This is the real secret of being eternally young.

Our profession has a deep impact on our subconscious mind. Till we study in college, our way of life is youthful, but as soon as we take on a profession of a doctor, engineer, manager or an entrepreneur and people subordinate to us give us respect, our views about ourselves change. We tend to feel like Bosses and assume a false persona (personal is a Greek word which means mask). Gradually this mask (or persona) becomes such an inseparable part of our personality that it leaves a deep impact on the subconscious mind. Our mannerisms and behaviour change to match with the characteristics of the persona that we have assumed.

Consequently, even if we are deprived of the earlier post or status, the effect continues to prevail. That is why mostly people, even after retirement, behave in haughty manner and try to project that they still hold a key position in the society. It is a very risky conditioning. On the contrary, those who are in service, suffer from the conditioning of obeying orders and sycophancy, as they have done during the time of their service.

Likewise, saints, sages and spiritual Gurus also become a victim of the same kind of conditioning. The more respect they are given, the more habitual they become of receiving praises. This creates a precarious illusion-net. A little praise and a small number of followers create an impression in their minds that the whole world follows them. The bigger the crowd, the stronger is the trap! They themselves do not come to know as to when they get caught in this vicious net. This illusion is nurtured by all leaders, Gurus, teachers, saints and they behave within the iambic of this assumed persona. An enlightened person, first and the foremost, gets rid of this false mask.

Therefore, it is important that whatever heights of success you may assume in life you must always try and preserve the child-like innocence of yours. You must remember to drop the garb of your professional status and position before entering the house. Live your profession as an act of play just like an actor is aware of the fact that he is not the real character but is merely playing the role of a character.

A man should live life like a play in a theatre and an actor should play his role like a real life situation. The sole secret of maintaining youthfulness is to preserve your innate child-like nature and live innocently like a child. Imagine yourself to be a child you will soon find that your subconscious mind will make you playful and youthful like a child. The more room you give to your ego, the earlier you will become old. Ego implies early old age and childish innocence means eternal youth.

Austerity is the Enemy of Youth

Austerity means the feeling of detachment from any object or person. It happens due to either over indulgence or enlightenment. One who practices overindulgence gets bored with it and soon gets detached from that object or person. However, such a person will try to find the same pleasure in some other object or person, maybe in the spiritual world. So basically, his object of pursue and focus changes but he remains attached to something or the other. Earlier he was busy eating, drinking, making merry and enjoying all the pleasures of life, but now his lifestyle changes and he likes living simply, abstinence, wearing plain

clothes, keeping fasts, eating boiled food, avoiding worldly talks, etc. It is important here to remember that the inner person is still the same. The only difference is that earlier he was living a worldly life in an ignorant manner, and now he is into spiritualism. But the point is that he is still ignorant because after some time, maybe in a couple of years, he will start detesting the spiritual lifestyle also. This way of life will appear dull and unexciting to him. Now he would again start thinking about the previous lifestyle and that would appear better to him. Like this, man often oscillates like a pendulum between the two different extremes of life – indulgence and austerity. This shows that austerity is a pretense.

An ordinary person enjoys everything in a state of unawareness and gets attached to whatever he comes in contact with and later that thing becomes boring and tasteless for him. On the contrary, an enlightened person lives in moderation and avoids the extremes of life. He lives in the present moment and does not get attached to the memories of the past or the dreams of the future. He does not oppose any kind of taste and enjoys whatever life offers him. Such a person is the true austere. The austerity of extremes develops when there are deep and fond memories of the past and a scale to measure the future. Austerity is the evidence of attachment with the past.

An enlightened person never talks of austerity. According to him every moment should be enjoyed but no memory of it should be retained. Enjoy and forget. Do not let the memories create a conditioning of the subconscious mind. If this happens, then real austerity emerges in life.

Therefore, do not let false austerity overwhelm your life. Live every moment of your life fully, take interest in everything and every person, dreams and desire, remain unsatisfied and strive to achieve more and create more. This is essential to keep your life active and moving. In order to remain young, you must take interest in all spheres of life.

Live with the principle of *satyam, shivam, sundaram*. Decorate your life, wear good clothes, look smart, enjoy the pleasures of life, put your sense organs to good use, utilise facilities and gifts of Nature, make progress, improve yourself and let your personality blossom fully. The nectar of bliss should trickle from each moment of your life. Enjoy everything but do not create memory of it and do not get attached to it. This is real spirituality, real establishment of *satyam, shivam, sundaram* and the secret of eternal youth.

□

How to Use the Subconscious Mind

We have understood two basic principles on which the subconscious mind works – ***repetition of a thought makes it a part (habit) of our subconscious mind and subconscious mind does not differentiate between truth and imagination.*** By using these two principles, we can bring change in our habits, develop new habits, transform our personality and accomplish impossible tasks.

Determine the kind of change desired – Confusion is weakness and habit of the human mind. When we wish to bring about a change, several types of conflicting thoughts cross our minds. Lack of any single and powerful thought causes the subconscious mind to remain unaffected. Therefore, first of all, clearly determine the change that you wish to bring in your life or behaviour. Write it on a paper.

Write the affirmation in present tense and not future tense – Whatever affirmation you wish to write, do it in present tense. For example, if you lack self-confidence and wish to increase it, then you must write: **"I am full of self-confidence."** You should NOT write, "I will be full of self-confidence." If your memory is weak, write: "I have a very strong memory." If you are physically weak, write: "I am strong, energetic and powerful." If you get up late in the morning, write: "I get up daily at 5 am sharp and finish all my work." You must never write, "Oh God, kindly improve my memory or give me confidence!" These are statements of the future tense, not present tense. The subconscious mind treats the statement of future tense like the future. The subconscious mind reads these statements as – At present, my memory is poor and I lack self-confidence. This leads to an incorrect programming of the mind and thus your wishes will never come true. On the other hand if you create an impression that the desired change has already come in your life, then the subconscious mind will accept your imagination as real and start building that type of energy for you.

Never write negative statements – Suppose, you want to control your anger, and you write a negative statement like, "Now I do not get angry" then basically, you are repeating and emphasizing the feeling of anger and the emotion of peaceful behaviour, or non-reaction has not been mentioned in the statement. When you think about anger, it will only cause anger and if you think about peaceful and clam behaviour, it will be realized. Never write: "I am not weak." The opposite of 'weak' is 'strong', so always write: **"I am strong and powerful."** Therefore, for very negative habit or emotion, write the opposite of it in a positive manner. **Write whatever you desire;**

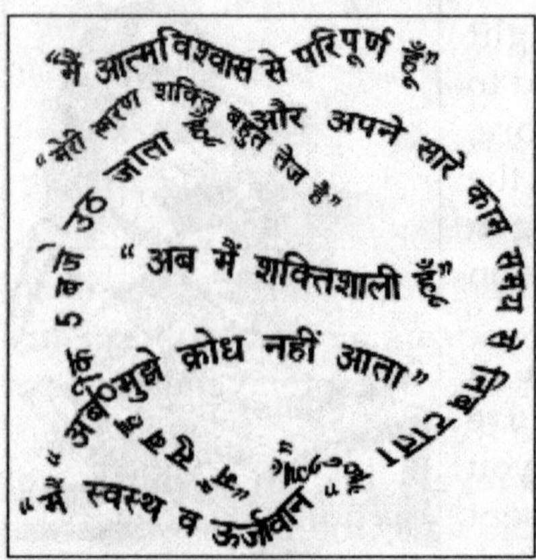

never write what you do not want because wherever we focus, energy expands and starts flowing in that direction. If we say that we do not want poverty and pain, the thought that intensifies is focused on poverty and pain. Consequently, we invite more poverty and pain in life. Opposites of poverty and pain are prosperity and happiness. Therefore, we need to focus on prosperity and happiness. This will make the energy flow in the desired direction and help us to invite these things in life. Unfortunately, we tend to focus and always think about the problems in our life. We rarely focus on the positive things of life and this in turn leads to more misery and pain. I have earlier mentioned that **everything in this world is governed by the Laws of Nature, and there is nobody here to make your destiny.**

When you write your desire on the paper, it takes a definite form and the uncertainty in the thought disappears. Therefore, writing an affirmation is very important.

Relax the body – In order to activate the subconscious mind, we have to free ourselves from the bondage of two things – our body and our conscious mind. Unless these two remain active, the subconscious mind fails to get activated. Once the body and the conscious mind are relaxed, the subconscious mind becomes fully active. To relax the body, you have to first relax the mind for which you have to go into the Alfa level.

How to achieve the Alfa level – Like the technique of ECG is used to measure heartbeats, the brain waves are measured by EEG (Electro Encephalograph). There are four types of states of our mind – Beta, Alfa, Theta and Delta states.

- **Beta State** – During this phase, our brain is fully active and the number of waves moving in the brain is 20-24 per minute. This is the state of complete awareness.
- **Alfa State** – During this state, our brain is slightly relaxed and the number of waves in the brain is 8-15 per minute. The mind is partially active and partially inactive i.e. the state of partial consciousness.
- **Theta State** – In this state the mind is completely relaxed and we fall asleep. The number of brain waves comes down to 5-8 per minute. It is the state of sleep and a person is said to see dreams in this state. In this state, we are very near to the subconscious mind.
- **Delta State** – In this, we pass into a state of deep sleep. The number of brain waves is further reduced to 3-5 per minute. It is the state of unconsciousness. Out of a total sleeping time of 8 hours, the mind remains in the Delta stet for nearly 2 hours only. There are no dreams in this state and the subconscious mind becomes completely inactive.

For our purpose, the Beta and the Delta states are of no use. Alfa state is sufficient to give instructions to the subconscious mind. Even the Alfa state has two levels – inner and outer. While in the outer level, the conscious mind is slightly active and it is used to change habits, fulfil desires, change mental states, control physical ailments, hypnotize and to accept any kind of suggestion. It is that kind of semi-conscious state where you can easily use the instructions given by your Master to affect your subconscious mind. If the conscious mind is not slightly active in this state, you will not be able to receive the suggestions given by your

Master. In order to go into this Alfa state, the body is not needed to be completely relaxed. A slight relaxation is sufficient to go into this state as our conscious mind is about 50% active in this state.

We get freed from our conscious mind in the inner level of the Alfa state. It is the deepest state of meditation. In this the conscious mind is only 10% active only to receive and follow the instructions of the Master. Our logical mind goes in a deep sleep and it is a state in which our astral body can come out of our physical body and go to any place and any time in the space. Travelling in the past or future is only possible in this level of the Alfa state. The astral body is then able to see all the events of the past and future as if witnessing a film on a screen. We can even see the events happening at that moment in our house, shop or at any place that we desire. We can also unravel the truths about theft, accidents and other secrets. I have used this technique for the Forensic department, CBI and even for the Press.

Basic Mental Waves

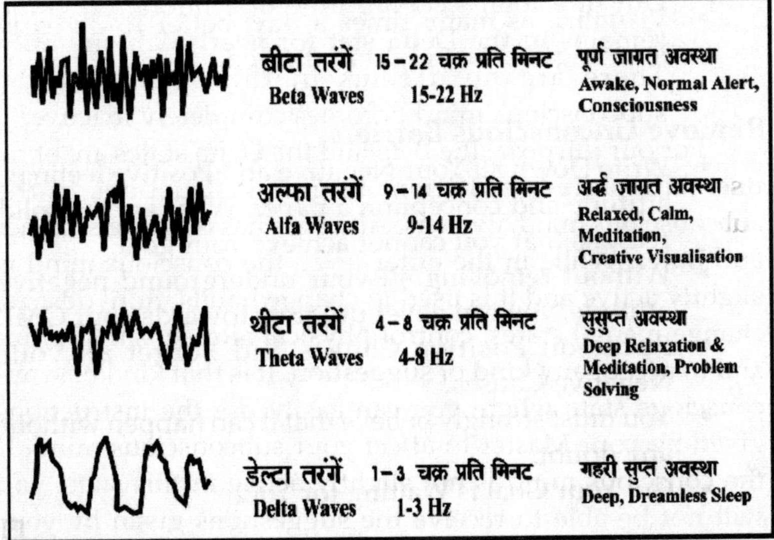

Definite
Goal Manifestation

- Decide What Exactly You Want.
- Write Down Your Specific Goal.
- Always Write in Present Tense, as though it is achieved.
- Add Emotional, Encouraging words.
- Visualize the End Result as a Reality.
- Visualize as many times a day; better to do early morning and late night in the bed.

Remove Unconscious Barriers

- Write Down all Your Negative and Positive feelings, attitude and conception a paper. What are the solid reasons that you cannot achieve your goal.
- Without removing all your underground negative attitude, you can never progress towards your Goal.
- Focus on Positive Causes and Forget all your Negative Causes.
- You must strongly believe that it can happen without any doubt.
- Go! Your Goal is Waiting for You.

□

The Technique of Alfa Level

Whenever Our Eyelids become Heavier, We Enter into Alfa State

As soon as our eyelids become heavy, it is the onset of the Alfa level. You must have noticed that in our everyday life when you get bored, your eyes begin to feel heavy and you feel sleepy. It is the semi-conscious or partial sleep state. You will also realize that while in this state, there are no thoughts in our minds. As our conscious mind becomes inactive, the thoughts disappear.

Thoughts occur in the mind only during two state – Beta (state of anxiety) and Theta level when the thoughts start pouring in the form of dreams. Therefore Alfa state is a type of state of thoughtless meditation.

Whenever you are in Deep Imagination, You Enter into Alfa State

You must have noticed that whenever you are into deep imagination, you do not seem to notice the sounds or the people around you. You come out from that state only when someone calls out to you loudly or brings you out of that state by physically touching you. You can call this as a kind of Alfa state because your mind, despite being conscious is not aware of your surroundings. It means that whenever we are in a state of deep imagination, we are in the Alfa state.

The below shows that there are mainly two rules of the Alfa state: (1) ***Make the eyelids heavy;*** and (2) ***Go into a state of deep and intense imagination.*** By keeping in mind these two basic rules, several methods can be used to go into Alfa level.

First Method: With open eyes, look at the agya chakra (the point between the eyebrows) with full force. Raise the eyeballs upwards so that the white portion of the eyes is visible more. Do not blink. While looking upwards between the brows, suggest yourself that by the count of ten, you will slip in the Alfa level. Then start counting backwards from ten and count it at such a pace that it should take around 3 minutes to count ten. As your eyes become heavy, feel your body getting heavy. Also feel the dizziness taking over your senses. See that you are getting drowned into the sea of tranquillity. Allow yourself to go into this state and keep suggesting your mind that you are going into the Alfa state. As your conscious mind begins to get inactive, your subconscious mind will get affected and create the desired state. As you finish the reverse counting, your conscious mind will become almost inactive though you will continue to hear all sounds around you. However, you feel the way you do when you get up in the morning wherein your body is heavy and mind is inactive yet aware of the surroundings. At this time, the subconscious mind is completely active and is ready to receive and accept any suggestion given to it.

Second Method: It is also called the 'Silva Mind' Method. It is the most widely used technique to control the mind. Relax yourself completely. Now start reverse counting from 100. If you wish, you can imagine a blackboard and see the numbers reducing gradually from 100 with each number appearing and then fading away slowly. During this exercise, the conscious mind is totally connected to the imagination. Reverse counting produces boredom in the mind, thus causing gradual heaviness. This leads to the conscious mind becoming inactive and enters into the state of semi-consciousness. If required, you can continue the counting till 50, then 20, 10 and 1. Till this time, the mind becomes accustomed to accepting the reverse counting.

Third Method: In this method, the body is first relaxed and then with closed eyes, you can look between the brows and imagine yourself entering into a dark cave. See yourself moving in a fast airplane in this cave which is studded with blue stones. Gradually you come across the first milestone on which number 10 is written. After crossing it, you see the next milestone of with number 9 written on it. The time gap between the appearing of these milestones may be around 10 seconds. If the mind is too active, you may increase the time gap from 20 to 25 seconds also. Likewise, slowly the milestones appear and the numbers keep reducing till 1. With the count of 1, you move from the realms of the conscious mind to the subconscious mind. The dark cave with black colour inside swiftly makes the mind inactive. The atmosphere inside the cave helps in making the mind inactive and helping it to quickly induce sleep. Such imaginations have a great impact on the mind.

Fourth Method: In this method, the body is made to relax. Thereafter, with the closed eyes, you should imagine yourself going down the stairs instead of the dark cave. These stairs take you to an unknown world or inside the temple of our God. Walk down each stair after a gap of 5 to 10 seconds. By the count of 1, you will reach the depths of the subconscious mind.

Fifth Method: In this technique, after relaxing the body, instead of going in a dark cave or going down the stairs, you can imagine dense black clouds or smoke. Beyond these clouds of smoke is the world of the subconscious mind. You should enter into the clouds and remain inside these clouds while counting from 10 to 1 in a span of 3 minutes. By the time you come out the clouds at the count of 1, you will come in the world of the subconscious mind.

Sixth Method: Chanting of any mantra is the easiest way to go in the Alfa level. You should chant any mantra in which you have absolute faith for a period of 5 minutes with complete concentration. Owing to its habit of being restless, the mind will begin to wander. Therefore, to control it, you can chant the mantra in a louder voice also. This can also help you in going into the Alfa level slowly. By meditating over your God, you can quickly reach the Alfa state.

Do Intense and Emotional Visualization

By making use of any of the methods described above, you can reach the Alfa state of mind. Now with all your emotion, imagine about the end result in the present scenario as if you have already acquired what you desire. You must visualize all the related events in a sequential manner leading to the end result of your choice. For example, suppose you wish to control your habit of overeating and reduce your weight. Then you must visualize that you have come to a dinner party where there are various types of dishes and excellent food. Your friends are pressing upon you to eat all those dishes, but you have bluntly refused those dishes. Instead, you are proceeding towards the stall of fruits and juice and that you have chosen to eat only healthy food (though in real life you love to eat delicious and all kinds of food). You have to also visualize that you are eating in less quantity and chewing the food properly (though in reality, you eat a lot and eat quickly without properly chewing). Then you visualize that your weight has reduced and your friends are congratulating you on your success.

Suppose you are short-tempered and impulsive. You react quickly and get annoyed at minor issues. If you wish to control your anger and change your habit, no amount of conscious control will bring about this change unless you make the changes at the subconscious level. It should be remembered that anger is generated from the subconscious mind. You will also agree that in the state of anger your conscious thinking becomes blurred and you are unable to think logically. In such an angry state, since your conscious mind is not working, you tend to react as per the wishes of your subconscious mind.

You have unknowingly created and established a subtle feeling, an emotion a form of ego in you and therefore, whenever a cause of anger appears before you, the conscious mind falls prey to it and fails to react as per your desire. If you wish to get rid of the emotion of anger, then forget the conscious mind and relax your body. Then go into the Alfa state and imagine yourself in those circumstances in which usually you get angry. In such a situation, imagine yourself to be calm, peaceful and happy. See yourself controlled and composed (tough in real life it is not so and you get very angry in such circumstances). Like this, you have to see yourself reacting opposite to your usual nature. Summarily, by regularly practicing and visualizing, you have to make your subconscious mind believe that you are a calm and composed person and that you have actually become so. Imagine all your family members, relatives and friends getting amazed at this change in you. Feel that they are admiring you for this positive change in your personality. Owing to this change, see your life and all its aspects change favourably and positively. Repeated visualization will do a programming inside your subconscious mind. As soon as the subconscious mind accepts this new conditioning, your behaviour will actually change and you will actually find yourself transformed into a calm and composed person. Now you must have understood that how do we use the subconscious mind to change our habits or nature.

Imagine yourself having the qualities which you currently do not possess: Do you feel that you do not possess the qualities of a specific salesman and that you are a bit reserved and shy? Do you wish to bring the qualities of that salesman in you? The first thing you need to do is to get rid of the feeling that you cannot become like him. In order to program your subconscious mind, first you will have to develop this conviction that you can develop those qualities with the help of your subconscious mind.

To begin with, note down on paper those qualities of the salesman which you would like to inculcate in yourself and write down that you have those qualities in you also. Now imagine that just in contrast to your present nature, you are talking freely to your customer and he is getting impressed with your talks. See yourself as an expert salesman who is able to sell his products in an impressive and effective manner and that you have rose very well in your career. You are being praised by everyone and that you have become extremely dynamic. Like this, you can easily develop various types of qualities within you. Therefore, as stated earlier, you have to feel that whatever change in habits and behaviour you wish to bring about in your personality, it has taken place and you are living happily with that change.

Do not let negative emotions hinder your path: It is seen that all day you create a negative programming in your mind that how is this particular thing possible? How is this change possible? I am not sure if it will change or not. These are such old and strong habits; how will I get new habits? What is to be shall be. Habits and nature continue till death. I am destined to be like this. The other person is blessed; how can I get those qualities? We are human beings so it is quite natural to have minor shortcomings, such as greed and anger etc. Such type of negative and depressing concepts and thoughts can put a break on your progress towards the new programming. These will not let positive and good emotions to build up within you. Therefore whenever you face negative emotions, you must overcome them with positive and intense thoughts. Imagine your mind to be filled only with positive emotions and feel yourself moving towards prosperity, growth and peace. Do not say that you do not get negative thoughts because when you say this, you are actually focusing on the negative thoughts. **Always remember that you should imagine what you want in your life and you should never focus on what you do not want in your life.**

Therefore, before imagining or visualizing on any other thought, you should first try to change your negative emotion and habits otherwise, your efforts to change the thoughts will not yield any result.

Practice for 21 to 30 days: You should practice the above-mentioned techniques of meditation for at least 21 to 30 days because during this period, the subconscious mind becomes receptive to your thoughts and commands and starts to bring about the desired change. Here, two principles come into play: **First,** through repetition, any thought and imagination can be made an integral part of the mind and starts manifesting itself in the form of a new habit. **Second,** subconscious mind believes your imagination to be true and starts bringing about the changes in the body chemistry and hormones and it sends similar type of vibrations in the Universe, thus receives the matching vibrations from the Universe. The greatest and the most powerful transmitter in the Universe is our subconscious mind which is capable of transmitting our thoughts at an unbelievable speed anywhere in the Universe beyond time and space.

□

All Wish Fulfillments are Deceptions

A common practice, not just in India but world over, is to have wish and votive then to please God after fulfillment of the desire by way of some special offerings, pilgrimages or other types of promises and conditions with God. We can call this a kind of spiritual bribe.

It is a major shortcoming of the human nature and it arises out of ignorance. We do not get this knowledge from any school or any teacher that man himself is a source of unlimited subtle powers using which man can produce vibrations of his choice and transmit them into the Universe to accomplish the desired goals and desires. Owing to this, man is devoid of the knowledge of the science and laws of subtle vibrations. Therefore, whenever he is faced with any hurdle or problem in life, he feels helpless. He supposes God to be an egoist businessman who can be pleased by a bit of flattery or accomplishing difficult tasks such as climbing mountains, keeping fasts. It is felt that all such feats can please the God and He fulfills our dreams and desires. Several people vow that they will practice celibacy or relinquish some of their favourite things like sugar, salt etc. It is an extremely dangerous and misleading conception of the mind.

There are several temples in India and abroad where people come from far off places to tie threads, offer water, milk or clothes thinking that this will help in fulfilling their desires. It is the ignorant thinking of the ignorant minds. This faulty thinking has been responsible for innumerable sacrifices of animals, hens, goats etc. performed all over the world and men do not hesitate to even put women folk live on the pyres of their dead husbands. The instances of sending one's wives to pundits and tantriks are common and the main driving force. All these misdemeanors is the thought that there is supreme egoist and sycophancy-loving power which is all powerful and which can be pleased by performing such frivolous acts of worship.

There is no gain saying the fact that if you ask people of any religion across the globe about the effect, these acts of worship have on their desired tasks and dreams, some will refuse to have got any results, some will acknowledge partial success, some complete success and some will say that they still have hope and faith that one day their desires will be fulfilled. Now the question arises that who decides their success or failure? Who is the main driving force behind all this? Is it God or some other force? The reply is that it is your subconscious mind. There has been an extreme ignorance as regards the knowledge of powers of the subconscious mind due to which success and failure of all tasks has been attributed to God alone. Even today the saints and ascetics are unaware of these powers of the subconscious mind and they are still asking people to blindly chant God's name, please Him and offer Him whatever they can. They propagate the concepts that a pilgrimage to a place will give the desired results. If the modern saints have been aware of the powers of the subconscious mind they would have never shared such misleading and incorrect principles with the public. However, there are several saints and Gurus who are well aware of these powers and they are introducing people to these powers.

God has made the Laws and Gone to Sleep

Since time immemorial, people have been nurturing a misconception that there is a crazy power called God who lives up in the sky. Sometimes He causes tsunami, at other times. He causes earthquakes and He even assists the terrorists who then create turmoil in countries. He is responsible for making a person rich or poor. He has made India poor, while He has bestowed immense wealth and prosperity on America, Europe etc. Despite being a witness to various kinds of inequality and discrimination, man has not yet been able to conclude that this world is not being governed by a single power called God, but is being run on the Laws made by Him. God has made these laws and has gone into deep slumber. He does nothing. He is interested in neither making anyone healthy and rich nor anybody poor and sick. He neither makes nor mars anyone's destiny. Everything happens here under a set of definite and pre-defined rules. You may choose natural diet and live upto 500 years or you may consume *paan, gutka,* tobacco and die

in 25 years! It is all completely your wish; God is not concerned with it! I have said this in the form of a poem –

What the earth has to do with the seed
Whatever way may be sown the seed
It subsumes those qualities and values
And takes the flavour bitter or sweet

The Earth is the rule of Nature
Your acts are the seeds you sow
One seed yields a thousand fruits
Thousand fruits give lacs of seeds

Says 'Nand' nobody in the world
Bestows upon you heaven or hell
They both are creations of the self

Each moment as we sow the seeds
With behaviour, diet and thought
Each moment one sows a seed
Each seed thus yields the fruit
Nothing does happen in a day

Says 'Nand' that remain aware, and conscious each moment,
The seed sown this moment, will yield its fruit tomorrow.

□

17

God Alone is the Supreme Power

This entire existence is God alone. Everything is God. We all are His expressions and the prosperity all around is what we call God. Actually, it is not God but Godliness that exists everywhere. Our ego does not let us taste the sweetness of His existence. As we break the shackles of our image-oriented ego, we come near to God. Therefore, we need to change our perception of the God, free Him from blind faith and connect His existence with science and truth. We will have to respect the laws made by Him and establish the greatness of His creation.

God has nothing to do with your problems, desires, diseases or your life. As soon as you dedicate yourself towards any form of God (be it a mosque or temple or church), it activates your subconscious mind and your mind is then connected with the Universe. Now whatever intention you create with all the force and intensity of thoughts, and see your desires getting fulfilled with full faith and conviction, those vibrations affect the subconscious mind and begin to attract the desired things from the Universe.

Universe is a treasure of unlimited powers and prosperity. You can either choose to become a magnet and attract everything you want from the Universe or remain deprived of all the treasure due to lack of faith and absolute belief. The choice is completely yours. God is not concerned with it. Like the Sun shines equally over all. You may choose to open the doors and windows, come out in the open and enjoy the sun or you may close the doors and choose to sit inside – it is your choice, your decision. God will not stop you from doing either.

More than anyone, God is kind to takes care of us
He is there to give, one is who is ready may take it.

Whenever you keep a fast or pledge something, then the thought of achieving something remains in your mind throughout the day and those powerful thoughts and emotions affect your subconscious mind. All such vows, fasts and pledges give strength to your belief and desire and empower your emotions. That is why your dreams and desires succeed in affecting the subconscious mind and thus you are able to get the desired results. Therefore, it is clear that God has no role and no interest in fulfilling your desires; it is actually your subconscious mind which plays the pivotal role in accomplishing all these tasks.

The failure or success of your desires depends on their basis. If the driving force behind your desire is greed, fear, vested interest, violence, jealousy or the tendency to hurt somebody, then it implies that you have an inclination towards receiving and not giving. This gives a negative feedback to the subconscious mind that your motive behind the desire is more important than the desire itself. This leads to a situation where the subconscious mind takes your emotions casually and thus it is not fulfilled. On the contrary, if your desire is motivated by a positive feeling of love, affection, welfare, creating good environment etc. for which some amount of sacrifice is also required, then your subconscious mind accepts it readily because in this case, you are willing to sacrifice anything for the fulfillment of the desire and that your desire is more important than anything else. The mind goes on repeating the desire. This creates a powerful vibration in the Universe and both the rules of the subconscious mind get activated. Repetition of the thought creates the necessary conditioning. Thus the subconscious mind accepts the imagination to be true and starts attracting similar circumstances and people required for the fulfillment of the desire.

It is here important to understand that the subconscious mind does not distinguish between good and bad. It fulfills all those desires which are made with a devoted mind. If an evil man is ready to sacrifice everything for spreading hatred and violence in the world, he will succeed in doing so because the intensity of his thoughts and emotions is so powerful that the subconscious mind is bound to get affected by it and produce the desired results even if it entails harming the world order. The important thing is to know that for the subconscious mind, evil and good have no meaning as it understands only the emotions be it good or bad. When you create a positive thought, the message is sent to the subconscious mind and it results in positive changes in the hormones and chemistry of the body. This widens our aura. It is also important to remember that the subconscious mind accepts only those vibrations which are created for the present and not for future. **Our subconscious mind does not comprehend the future or the past. These exist only for the human beings. The subconscious mind only believes in the present tense.** If it would accept the future dreams also, all dreams and desires of lazy people would have been fulfilled by now without their having to do anything. Since all prayers and pledges are said in future tense, despite such a large of prayers said everyday by numerous people, there is no impact of these in the world and it leads to no change in the situation. Undoubtedly due to the good intentions, the effect of positive and healthy vibrations is created causing a mild effect. However, no significant result or change is seen because the vibrations related to the present tense which actually affects the subconscious mind and the Universe were never sent in to the Universe.

It is necessary to create all the prayers and thoughts in the present tense, such as, **"there is total peace in our life"** or **"there is complete peace in the world."** Instead of saying, "O God, please protect us", you must say, **"I am protected each moment."** Likewise, instead of saying, "Please bestow wisdom on me", you should say, **"I am wise and intelligent."** Therefore, all prayers and desires should be expressed in the present tense and also it is important to view and imagine the dreams to have been fulfilled. It is after doing so, the subconscious mind accepts your desire and sends positive vibrations into the Universe, thus attracting similar positive vibrations and helps in materializing our dreams. **'Like attracts like'**, is the principle which works in the case of energy. It is an undisputable Law of the Nature.

It is quite natural to dream for a happy and prosperous life, to have desires, to hope for a bright future and these desires have always found expression in the prayers said by human beings. In the past, the sages and ascetics were mostly ignorant of the powers of the subconscious mind and the principle on which it works, so they made prayers casually in future tense and since centuries we have been saying these prayers religiously though not much impact of these have been experienced by us.

Since times immemorial, man has been saying such prayers and believing in their usefulness. We all do it. But what happened? Where is the energy built by these prayers? Has the God become deaf that He does not listen to our prayer? Had these powerful prayers been said correctly with the right amount of energy, there could have been enormous positive and healthy changes in the world till now. We would have been living in an environment rich in resources. However, the situation of the environment and our surroundings is pathetic today. We have been living and hoping for a good future, whereas we need prayers for the present times. The Laws of the Universe and the subconscious mind do not accept any vibration other than those related to the present tense. Therefore, there is a need to redraft and change the prayers and the way they are said so that they become present-oriented. If we say these prayers and express our desires powerfully in the present tense, the subconscious mind will surely accept them and believing them to be true, it will attract matching vibrations from the Universe and fulfil all your dreams, wishes and desires.

□

18

How do Good and Bad Intentions Yield Results

We do not oblige or help anyone by keeping good or bad intentions. In fact, we help or harm ourselves by having these thoughts. Good thoughts are light and positive. As soon as we connect with thoughts, our body feels light and the aura begins to expand. On the contrary, the bad or evil thoughts make our body feel heavy and the aura contracts.

As we get associated with good thoughts (love, compassion, affection, kindness, cooperation, help, non-violence, egoless state of mind, charity, peace, humility, happiness, confidence, devotion, prayer, meditation, music etc.), our subconscious mind gets affected with these emotions and generates positive hormones in the body. This relaxes the nervous and cellular systems of the body, thus leading to excellent blood circulation. This in turn, causes the aura to expand and our magnetic effect increases. Due to this, our presence creates a positive impact on others. We begin to attract more life force from the Universe. This has a good effect on our body, mind and soul which then becomes the cause of a happy future. The lightness generated in the body owing to these positive thoughts makes us feel like jump, dance, sing, play and perform other such acts of happiness.

Contrary to the above, the negative emotions (hatred, jealousy, criticism, anger, frustration, fear, argument, violence, ego, irritability, etc.) affect the subconscious mind in a manner where it produces negative and harmful hormones in the body. This leads to the body systems getting tensed and thus the blood circulation is adversely affected. The aura thus contracts. A weak aura is unable to defend against the various kinds of negative energies from Universe. This causes immense harm to the body, mind and soul. This invites diseases, bad luck and sorrow in our lives.

Therefore, the element that gets most affected by the good and bad emotions is our subconscious mind. It is unable to distinguish between the good and the bad. It simply accepts out thoughts and give results accordingly in the form of benefit or otherwise. The kind of thoughts we accept is therefore, our choice. A person who is unaware of these facts is likely to pick good as well as bad emotions. However, an aware person can choose to discard the negative feelings and accept only the positive emotions so that he is able to get complete advantage. As such, it is quite simple to make use of this spiritual reality and lead the life of your choice!

□

Good Qualities can also be Devastating

Yes, it may sound weird, but it is absolutely true. Virtues like truth, honesty, discipline, morality, etc. can devastate you and cause sorrow, pain and disease in your life. Those who are honest, do not rejoice in being honest, instead they fret about the dishonesty of others and keep complaining all day about it. They remain in deep sorrow and their life remains focused on such dishonest people. Despite being honest themselves, they are always in search of dishonesty among others. This causes more dishonesty to come in our lives. Since our focus is always on dishonesty, we emit similar vibrations all the time and consequently, attract more and more dishonest people around us, whereas we should always focus on honesty.

Those who are virtuous and truthful remain unhappy

due to falsehood of others. Such people, instead of enjoying their truthfulness, focus on the non-truthfulness of others and thus, invite more misery and distrust in their lives.

Likewise, disciplined people mostly focus on the indiscipline of others. This behaviour is extremely self-damaging as they are unable to change the attitude of others and in the process, cause damage to themselves. A disciplined person remains tensed and worried about the negative qualities in other people. He behaves angrily and becomes irritable whenever he comes across indiscipline anywhere in any form.

What we see in our imagination and think in our mind affects our subconscious mind. Despite being good and positive, if we focus on negative and evil behaviour of others then we will invite more pain, more misery and more negativity in our lives.

If a virtuous or an honest man feels somewhat superior to others and egoist, then this ego and complex also cause tension and grief because ego is a negative emotion for the body and as soon as the egoist emotions get associated with us, our aura contracts. Such a person gets locked and confined within the boundaries of his limiting thoughts. Under the effect of ego, he picks up quarrels, fights, arguments, tension and enmity. Therefore, as per the Laws of the Nature, his life always remains sorrowful and tensed.

If you are virtuous, pray to the Almighty that He may bestow a similar blissful life upon others. Those, who have an evil disposition, should control it by feeling of affection and compassion. It is good to guide their lives, make them aware, inspire them without compromising the bliss of your own life.

☐

Subconscious Mind: The Treasure-house of the Intuition

The best and the highest medium to the Space and the Universe is the subconscious mind. It is the only main centre to express the invisible and subtle energies of the Universe. With the help of this centre, we can see and feel the past and future energies, which are very much existent but invisible to the conscious mind and our sense organs. The technique of seeing the subtle energies is also known as Clairvoyance. We may also prefer to call it Divine Vision or the Third Eye. The technique of listening to the subtle sounds is known as Clairaudience. These sounds are heard through Intuition in the form of soft whispers by the divine souls.

You may be surprised to know but it is a fact that in all great inventions, discoveries and creations including works of art, literature, music, etc. the contribution of the conscious mind is limited; the main source of inspiration is the subconscious mind of the persons concerned. The conscious mind prepares a working ground but the real life and energy force is provided by the subconscious mind. Through our best possible conscious efforts, even if we prepare or create something, we usually realize in the end that the particular creation may be satisfactory but it is not outstanding and that it lacks the requisite liveliness; it is devoid of the fragrance of brilliance. Owing to the requirement of your job or any other compulsion, the work has to be completed somehow but such creations do not last long and lose their luster after some time. However, when you tend to abandon the work in between due to fatigue or boredom and your conscious mind does not cooperate much with you, then the subconscious mind, by way of intuition, attracts divine ideas from the Universe.

There are two ways of attracting divine creations from the Universe and in both these methods the conscious mind has to become inactive. First, when you are completely engrossed in your work and you lose track of time thus losing the desire to eat, drink or sleep, at his stage your conscious mind becomes inactive and all the ideas and inspirations are acquired through your subconscious mind. Second, when you feel exhausted and drained out with your conscious efforts and tend to leave everything to the will of God, then creative, innovative and divine ideas befall upon you from the Universe. All artistes, musicians, literatures, scientists, etc. invariably experience this divine help. Such creations and ideas received through intuition become masterpieces and are remembered for times to come. Here it is important to understand that behind this success of intuition, conscious mind also plays an important role because unless the conscious mind weaves a net of dreams and aspirations, the fish of intuition does not get trapped in that net. Therefore, intuition does not come on its own. Moreover, conscious mind should not strain itself to dream or aspire. In fact, dreams and aspirations should be natural. Gradually, as the time progresses and the more our desires become strong, the more intuition and divine guidance is bestowed upon us. Intuition does not become active without the active role of conscious mind.

The creative world of Intuition is unlimited. All inventions, discoveries and innovative and creative changes taking place in our society everyday bear testimony to this fact. Intuition is the natural ability of every human being. At every step in your life, the intuition – in the form of inner voice – guides you through visions, sounds and other related events. However, owing to your logic-dominated approach, you tend to ignore and suppress this inner voice. We all know that whenever we find ourselves at crossroads, the inner voice guides us and tell us to choose a particular course of action. However, we prefer suppressing the inner voice and thus, go by the logical mind and take decisions accordingly, only to realize later in life that those decision that we took against the inner voice proved wrong. We even say – 'I wish I paid heed to my inner voice'! The innocent and the God-fearing usually listen to their inner voice, whereas the educated lot prefers to go by the logic. There

are researches and records to prove that most great men achieved greatness because they listened to their inner voice rather than to their logical brain.

It is a fact that God, Nature and the Universe are anxious all the time to give you the correct guidance, but you are unable to free yourself from the logical and conscious mind. As soon as the feeling of absolute surrender gets into our being, intuition comes into action. Therefore the proper way is that you should dream and aspire and create vibrations with full intensity and conviction; along with this, you should also calm your mind, meditate and surrender your being to the will of God sincerely believing that the potential of the conscious mind is limited whereas that of the subconscious mind is unlimited. As such, at each opportune moment, a glimpse of intuition will shine within you and will guide you on the right path. It is to be believed that innocent people who have absolutely surrendered to the will of God make full use of the divine help and you will find them often saying that our God or Guru guide us at every step.

How to Recognize intuition

The term 'Intuition', refers to the guidance and thoughts which come from within the soul and where mind or logic have not been used, one which has its source in the subconscious and not in the conscious mind, and which originates in a calm state of mind. If you wish to solve any of the problems through divine intervention without application of your own mind, the let a strong desire grow inside you that you need divine guidance and then keep working with a peaceful mind. You should take care that you must neither wait for the guidance intentionally nor become restless during the process because the guidance is already within you; you have to only maintain quiet and patience for the intuition to rise to the fore. Only if you have faith and conviction, you will suddenly find a solution striking your mind, or the solution may appear in a dream, or a person may come in your contact who will lead you to the solution of the problem. This is not related to your destiny or God; it takes place strictly as per the Laws of Nature. While searching for the solution to a problem, if you get restless and anxious, your body and mind become tensed and the flow of natural forces get hindered, but when you surrender yourself to divine help, relax your mind and body then the natural forces freely flow through your being thus helping you to find the solution easily and quickly. Here, it is to be clearly understood that while it is important to have strong desire, anxiety and eagerness to find the solution, it is equally vital to maintain peace, calmness, surrender and a strong faith in the will of God because it is the right combination of both desire and faith that gives birth to intuition.

Gita, Quaran, Bible, Gurugranth Sahib, Dhammapadas, Upanishadas and all other such religious scriptures are not the result of the efforts of the conscious mind; they have found way through the powers of the subconscious mind. Lord Krishna, Buddha, Jesus, Nanak,

Prophet Muhammad etc. have all been pure and Godly media for these scriptures to appear because these souls had made their minds absolutely calm and they have allowed the intuition to flow freely through them.

Types of Intuition

There are several types of intuition and all these occur only through the subconscious mind.

Inner Vision

Every individual has the ability to see the past and the future. We all often experience that when some events occur in our life, we feel as if we have earlier seen or dreamt of these events earlier. Sometimes, a scene plays before our eyes that a particular event is about to happen. At that moment, you tend to ignore the thought as a figment of mind, but sometime later when that event actually takes place you say that you had already seen it happening earlier. If you happen to sit with a person – good or bad – you keep getting an inner guidance about that person or some events which are going to take place.

It often happen in Reiki (touch therapy) that while giving healing to a person whose is not getting relief in his disease, the healer sees the root cause of the disease (physical, mental, emotional, karmic, vastu, etc.) like a video playing in front of him. Often the elderly people like our parents, relatives or Gurus, while giving blessings see future scenes and give their blessings accordingly.

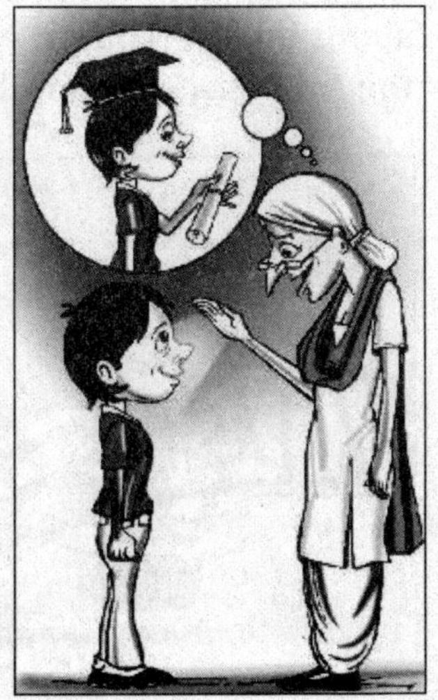

During Reiki treatment from a distance, the healers often give accurate descriptions of the present condition of the patient, status of the house, colour of clothes, and other surroundings. All these are examples of Inner Vision.

Precognition

Often people witness major events which are going to take place in the future such as a massive fire, accident, storm, cyclone, murder, theft etc. Though they are not directly connected to those events in any manner but they get a glimpse of those events. This is called Precognition. Rising above the physical world, we realise that the entire Universe is a nothing but a complex net of subtle energy forces. There are innumerable subtle thoughts and energy waves existing in the Universe. Our subconscious mind gets connected to any of these energy waves and we start getting information about events related to that energy. Since we are not directly related with that event, so we do not pay attention to it, but when after some time, when that event actually takes place, we realise what we had witnessed earlier was correct. With the help of meditation and strong desire, we can easily rise above the physical world and travel in the world of subtle energy forces and gather information about any person or event. And in all these activities, it is the subconscious mind which plays the most crucial role.

Psychometry

This is yet another form of intuition and inner vision. In this technique, when we hold an object in our hand and meditate with closed eyes and a peaceful mind, we see several visions and gather various kinds of information related to that object. Any object that you come in contact with be it land, house, cloth, or any other article, our subconscious mind gets connected to the events related to that object and provides you the information about it. People with such developed powers are known as 'psychiatrist' and their abilities are utilised by the police departments (CIA, FBI, KGB, etc.) in order to investigate crimes and gather information about crimes and criminals.

Tarot Card Reading
An Intuitional Guidance

There are 72 guide cards in Tarot pack and the Tarot Card Reader asks you to choose a certain number of cards from the pack. If the cards are chosen with efforts using the conscious mind, the prediction comes out to be incorrect, but if you surrender yourself to the will of god and make your mind calm and relaxed, your hands will automatically move towards the cards which are actually related to you. This happens due to the force of attraction between the cards and your subconscious mind. If a particular card is not right for you, then your hand despite going near to that card, will suddenly retreat and move towards the right card. Owing to this reason, successful Tarot Card Readers are very few because it is a highly developed technique which needs a lot of practice. Infect, the Tarot Card Readers appearing on TV are also fake and incorrect as they are quite active and conscious at that time, while the Tarot Card Reader also has to go into the Alfa level before pulling a card for you because it is only in such state that the subconscious

mind cooperates. Therefore, predictions of an illiterate, innocent and honest Tarot Card Reader tend to be much more accurate and authentic than those of an anxious, greedy and egoist Tarot Card Reader.

Astrology

Less of Mathematics, more of Intuition

Astrology is an ancient and complex science. We all will agree that predictions of 99 per cent astrologers are incorrect. The reason behind this inaccuracy is that their predictions are mostly based on mathematics and not on intuition. Earlier, spiritual practices were used in astrology, Tarot card reading, Crystal Ball Gazing, Dowsing etc. and some God or mantra etc. was used to intensify our emotions and feelings so as to enable the subconscious mind to attract special energy waves in the form of intuition. All processes and methods explained in our spiritual and religious scriptures are not aimed at showing a miracle, but their purpose is to develop strong feelings and emotions and enhance inner powers. When you sit in front of a God and chant some mantra, your conscious mind becomes relaxed. All such spiritual practices are meant to slow down the activity of mind. As your feelings and emotions get stronger, they begin to attract similar vibrations from the Universe. Intuition cannot be imposed; the more your mind gets relaxed, the more it begins to show and guide you. Therefore, ancient astrologers were not just educated but also spiritually evolved. Modern

astrologers are perhaps more educated and less spiritual. That is why their predictions do not come true. They are greedy and egoist and make use of the fear and weaknesses of the common man to their own advantage. True astrologers are rare.

Dowsing

The Simplest Way to Experience The Power of Subconscious Mind and Intuition

Dowsing is a technique of searching or finding the unknown. Several types of instruments (called dowsers) such as Pendulum, L-rods, Spring rod, etc. are used to find the answers. It is sometimes felt that the instruments used in dowsing are moved by the person doing the dowsing but here it is interesting to note that whatever instrument you use in dowsing, move automatically with varying speeds. Whenever a question is asked, the dowser moves in a particular type of motion with some speed. How is it possible? Why do these instruments move automatically on asking a question?

The fact is that in a relaxed mental state when you ask a question about any object – hidden water, a lost article, person or any other thing – the subconscious mind sends those energy waves in the Universe and then receives the matching energy waves (the answer to the question) from the Universe and transmits it to your body. However, the signal received from the subconscious mind is so subtle that an ordinary person is unable to read and analyse it. Therefore, dowsing instruments are used to further amplify this signal thus making it visible and easy to comprehend. Often the direction of movement of the dowser indicates the direction in which the lost article, person etc. could be found.

In this technique the conscious mind is a major hurdle. It should be used only to ask a question and then it should be made to relax because the answer has to be received by the subconscious mind. Usually what happens is that before the subconscious mind can receive the correct answer from the Universe, the conscious mind gets focused on some imaginary thought and the dowser starts moving as per the thought created by the conscious mind thus giving a wrong answer. The basic principle of dowsing is that the conscious mind should only ask the question and then it should go into a state of relaxation so that the subconscious mind can do it work effectively. There is nobody who can contact the Universe or the spiritual world except the subconscious mind. Therefore if the conscious mind is allowed to remain even slightly active, the subconscious mind will not be able to do its job freely. While the conscious mind remains in touch with the physical world, it is the subconscious mind that connects to the subtle world. So, in dowsing, we ask a question with the help of our conscious mind but then allow the subconscious mind to receive the answer.

The subconscious mind has an amazing power that depending on the intensity of your thought and emotion. It can come in contact with any energy wave in the Universe within a fraction of a second, which is why your body begins to receive the vibrations as soon as a question is asked and you are able to get the answer through the dowsing instrument. For example, as soon as you think of a person 'X', an image of that person is created in your mind and instantly energy waves are sent out in the Universe. Thereafter, if the conscious mind is in a relaxed state, the subconscious mind will start attracting energy vibrations related to 'X' and transmit them to your body. The next moment, if you think about 'water', your body will drop the vibration of 'X' and start attracting energy waves related to 'water' from the Universe. Likewise, as your thoughts change, the energy vibrations also change. This is how the exchange of energy waves takes place between your body and the Universe. It is also pertinent to mention here that this phenomenon of energy exchange takes place beyond the limitations of Time and Space. This is the reason why we are able to establish instant contact with any person/object anywhere in the Universe. How miraculous is the power of our subconscious mind!

□

Telepathy – Transmission of Thoughts

Telepathy is the technique of transmitting your thoughts, vibrations or emotions to any place to any person in the Universe. It is another miraculous power of the subconscious mind, that while sitting at our place we can connect to any place, person or thing in this Universe – a person, animals, plants even stars and planets. This power is also present in animals and birds. The only agent in this Universe having the ability to connect itself to the subtle world is the subconscious mind.

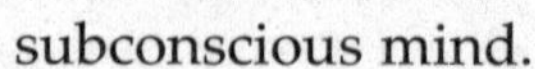

With the help of Telepathy, we can contact a person sitting miles away from us merely by way of intention. While sitting far away from a person, if we sincerely think about a person, our subconscious mind gets connected to the subconscious mind of that person and then whatever thoughts – positive or negative – you wish to project in his mind, should be clearly visualized by you. This will slowly cause the same thought pattern to be created in the mind of that person also. As those thoughts become powerful in your mind, its effect is created in that person's mind as well and those thoughts tend to dominate over his conscious mind and logic. The harder the conscious mind, the tougher and longer it becomes to affect it. Weak minds are usually affected early. Therefore, with the help of telepathy, we bring about positive and desired changes in our surroundings, relations and circumstances. Sincere prayers and well-wishes exhibit a positive effect due to telepathy. *Tantriks* also use telepathy to transmit negative thoughts and destructive energy waves across to the target person. As such, all prayers (positive) and tantrik practices (negative) become successful due to the process of telepathy, which is actually a power of the subconscious mind.

In all the distance healing practices like Reiki, Pranic (प्राणिक) Healing, Dowsing, Crystal Science etc., the principle of Telepathy is used to transmit the healing energy across to the person requiring the healing thus it cures the person of physical, mental, psychic and other emotional ailments. There is absolutely no difference in giving healing to the patient from a distance and in-person. In fact, during from a distance, the healing process is often finished in a few seconds whereas in-person healing may require longer because during distance healing, the energy travels at a subtle level and works at an amazingly fast speed. This fact has been successfully proved by innumerable Reiki practitioners across the globe.

Connect anywhere in the Universe with Telepathy

Through Telepathy, we can clear our past life *karmas* and we can also send positive energy in the future to build a bright and prosperous future for ourselves. While one person can send positive energy to another and heal him, hundreds of people can jointly heal the entire world and bring about a positive transformation because when such a huge amount of positive energy is created, it is bound to show its effect in the world; such a massive mass of energy cannot disappear unnoticed!

A research is going on in the American Army as to how messages can be coded and decoded with the use of Telepathy without actually taking the help of any telecommunication devices.

It implies that with the help of Telepathy, we can, beyond the boundaries of time and space, establish contact with past and future events of our life and bring about desired changes in the circumstances to change our destiny. Telepathy is capable of contacting any person, thing, situation or event in the Universe within seconds in accordance with the thoughts and emotions occurring in our mind.

With the help of Telepathy, you can charge water from a distance, treat and heal animals, birds, plants, human beings and perform many other such tasks by having access to the world of subtle energies.

□

22

Science of Hypnotism – A Trick of the Subconscious Mind

The science of hypnotism is solely dependent on the power of the subconscious mind. In this, the conscious mind is made to relax using several techniques and then the subconscious mind is given suggestions to solve any physical, mental or emotional problem of a person. Any positive change can surely be brought about by this technique. Our habits, fears, misunderstandings, mental blockages, complexities, misconceptions etc. exist at the level of the subconscious mind. However hard we may try but it is not possible to get rid of these problems using our conscious mind. The only tool available to us

is our Will Power though it is only capable of putting a temporary break on these problems. Once the grip of will power loosens, our problems tend to resurface. However, these problems continue to exist inside our subconscious mind and due to the will power of the conscious mind they remain subdued. This causes an unending inner conflict and tension. Through hypnotism, you can easily connect with the subconscious mind and give suggestions to get rid of these fears and problems permanently. Today, Hypnotism is recognized world over by the medical doctors as an alternative therapy for treatment. **I personally believe that without the knowledge of the science of hypnotism, every physician – from any stream of medicine – is incomplete.** More than 90% of our life is governed by the make-up of our subconscious mind. You can transform your life completely either by self-hypnotism or by taking the help of a specialist of this field.

Once the conscious mind goes into the state of deep relaxation, the subconscious mind can be given any suggestion and the subconscious mind is then bound to follow it. In the state of hypnotism, if you suggest that your hand has become numb and that it has lost all sensation, your hand will actually become numb and senseless. Now, even if the hand is cut or pierced, you won't feel any pain! If you suggest that your hands have got stuck, you won't be actually able to separate them! If it is suggested that you are an infant and you are hungry, then you will really start crying for milk and behave like an infant!

By now, you understand very well that the subconscious mind does not go by logic and it never contradicts you or opposes anything you suggest; it simply accepts your command and executes them meticulously. Therefore, any suggestion given to it by way of imagination is considered true by the subconscious mind and then it will bring about exactly the desired kind of physical or mental change in you. How miraculous is our subconscious mind!

□

Subconscious Mind can take us into the Past and Future Lives

It has been explained earlier that our subconscious mind is connected with the energies of the Universe and it can reach out to any point of time beyond the boundaries of time and space. It is capable of witnessing thousands of years of the past and future because the realization of time and space exists only for the physical world and conscious mind, not for the subconscious mind. Therefore, whenever a person goes into a state of deep meditation, he is said to have gone beyond time, space and emotions. Time is actually an illusion. Since everything in this Universe is moving and changing each moment, it is only felt that time is moving. However, in the depths of meditation,

this realization disappears. A long spell of meditation may also seem like that of a short duration of a few minutes.

Using the technique of hypnotism, we can easily take a person into Alfa and Theta levels thereby make him see the events of past and future, wherein he can witness each and every event of the past and future lives like a video film. A person, while seeing the past lives, can even see the exact reasons of pain and misery in his present life and accordingly, rectify his mistakes of the past or make necessary changes in his behaviour in order to lead a happy and prosperous life. After going into the past or the future life, there is need for you to study the scriptures because these scriptures are tread at the level of the mind and remains limited at the level of the mind only which is in fact of no value as it is an experience of some other person. Since it is not your own experience, the knowledge acquired remains at the superficial level of your being. However, when we ourselves go into the past and future lives, it serves as an eye opener and we get to know the truth of life, soul and other such concepts. This has even lead to the state of enlightenment in some cases. It is a knowledge which cannot be given to you by any scripture or any Guru or Mahatma. Therefore, travelling into your past and future lives is an experience which is equivalent to experiencing life, laws of God and truth and giving a positive turn to your entire life.

Our subconscious mind records each and every event of all our past and future lives, along with every memory, every *samskara* and as it gets revealed to you during the past and future life travels, they leave you completely surprised and speechless!

Narco Test

A Unique Method of Checking the Crime

In the famous Narco test, the conscious mind of a criminal is put to rest by giving him a heavy sedative and thereafter, all the secrets and truth is revealed from his

subconscious mind by asking various types of questions. The criminal gives absolutely correct answers to all the questions without using any logic and reasoning. These answers and information revealed during the course of Narco interrogation give major breakthrough in solving criminal cases. Therefore, the entire procedure of Narco Test is based on utilizing the potential of subconscious mind.

In Drunken State a Person Always Speaks the Truth

When a person is in a drunken state, the alcohol in his body gradually subdues his conscious mind and then he

loses the power to use his logic and reasoning. In such a state, subconscious mind brings his suppressed emotions and feelings to the fore and so he starts speaking the truth. That state reveals the true state of the person. The way of living that we normally exhibit is not our true self; it is nothing but a mask. The real self is revealed only when the conscious mind gets subdued and the subconscious mind becomes active. Therefore, only the people who are close to us get to see our true self.

Whenever people tell me that 'Sharmaji, you are an excellent human being, a great man indeed', I often reply, 'First you go and ask my wife, my children and my staff. If

they also say that I am a good human being only then you must believe it, otherwise not.' It is because what we appear to others is only our outer being; the real being, the inside still remains hidden. As such, every individual in this world lives with two different personalities – one is the outer one which is seen by others and the other our real self which remain hidden from general public. This real self begins to show itself in the times of crises and problems or when we are at the crossroads of life, when we have make critical choices in life, when we fall sick and are faced with difficult situations. The revelation of this true personality can leave the people around us completely surprised as they happen to see this aspect of our personality for the first time.

The barrier between the conscious and the subconscious mind can be shattered by meditation which then leads to true knowledge and enlightenment. Such enlightened souls have one personality. There is no difference between their outer and inner self. They are devoid of a past or future; they live in the present moment. He travels in the past and the future at his will. His conscious and the subconscious mind do not control his behaviour. In fact, he controls his conscious and subconscious minds. During excited states such as joy, grief, fear or anger, our conscious mind becomes inactive and the subconscious mind takes over. I have said it in a poem like this –

Do not send anger out of your life,
Anger has lead to great miracles.

Man speaks the truth when angry,
and reveals the secrets of his heart.
He weighs the pros and cons of life,
And anger shows the real face of all.
Here each one is deceiving another,
But anger unveils the true relations.
Anger can tell a saint from a fraud,
Anger, says 'Nand', incites the ego.

□

Why do Our Pilgrimages, Worships, Charities, Yagyas Yield no Success

Since time immemorial, Man has been looking for new ways and methods to please God and fulfil his dreams and desires such as keeping fasts, performing yagyas, walking barefoot, observing silence, pilgrimage etc. The basic reasons all these activities is to please God. At a superficial level though all these things appear to be good and pleasing but at the core of it, lies fear, greed and sycophancy, the desire to attain success and satisfy one's ego. Your subconscious mind catches the deep-lying hidden desires and howsoever your activates may appear pure and worthwhile but the truth is the basic thoughts behind all this pretense are negative. The subconscious mind focuses on what is true and your real self and transmits only those kind of vibrations in the Universe and thus attracts the matching vibrations back from the Universe. Owing to this fact, instead of getting positive results, you tend to get only negative outcomes.

There is no gain in saying the fact that nobody actually wants to keep fasts, walk barefoot or observe silence. But somewhere there is a feeling hidden deep in their psyche which causes the statement to get repeated, "I do not want to face this crisis, but what to do, I am helpless! In order to get rid of the problems, I will have to do this!" Therefore, the basically it is not the willingness to do something positive,; it is just a self-imposed compulsion. However, the subconscious mind is able to see through the pretense and it knows your true self very well. Some people, often, in order to prove themselves to the real and true devotees of the God, repeatedly perform various kinds of religious and spiritual practices. But the subconscious mind only pays attention to the egoist feeling inside such people and creates matching vibrations. Therefore, despite repeating such practices and performing all kinds of *pujas*, etc. such persons fail to get any peace, joy and prosperity because their underlying thought is fraught with ego, greed, sycophancy and fear. This causes only negative results to appear in his life.

I have earlier clarified this fact that God has made the rules and has gone to sleep. He does not do anything now and everything is governed by the indisputable laws of Nature framed by God. If despite pilgrimages, worships, charities, yagyas, you fail to get any worthwhile result, then rest assured that your basic thought process is not correct and your intentions do not match with the Laws of Nature.

It is the same with charity. If you consider charity to be an investment with the Almighty with a hope that a rupee given in charity will come back to you in lakhs then your charity is nothing but an act of greed. If you give charity with the hope of getting a place in heaven or better life, then also your charity is based on greed.

Some people give charity merely to get

rid of their black money which cannot be utilised in any way other. So instead of getting into the mess of income tax, they donate it to some temple or give it in charity. Since here again the intention is not to actually give the money in charity but to save oneself from tussles and problems, thus the result will also be negative. If you really intent to get a positive and pure outcome, your acts should be inspired by compassion, gratitude, love, affection and well-being of others. In charity, the most significant thing is not the amount but the feeling and intention with which the charity is done. Even a 10-rupee note given with positive and good intention will give more positive reward than one crore rupees given with a feeling of either greed or with some other ulterior motive. Therefore the result depends not on the amount but the feeling with which the money is donated. Our subconscious mind also works on this principle; it favours only the truth. It is a misconception of our egoist mind that thinks if we give more money then God will treat as in some special manner and consider as VIP. However, the subconscious mind and God both give importance to our intentions and not to our superficial acts of charity.

If you donate money to create a social image for yourself and enhance your ego among your friends and relatives that people will consider you to be extremely kind, benevolent, then your real intention is that of ego and greed. In that case, no power of this Universe can give any positive result to you. This may lead to some temporary moments of pleasure but eventually it will yield only negative outcome because the intention (i.e. the seed of the act) is wrong.

If you are donating money with a feeling that you are superior to the person receiving the money, then also there is an egoist intention hidden behind the act. This will again give a negative output. Therefore, in order to avoid this intention, the word *'dakshina'* is used India. It has an implicit meaning that the giver is filled with gratitude towards the received that the latter is gladly receiving the donation.

If, while giving donations, you keep an account of it and expect any favour in return then your charity is nothing more than a form of beggary, a demand, a sort of greed. And you will get the result in accordance with these feelings. Eventually the result is negative which naturally does not meet your expectations.

Misuse of Fasts

Fast is the English term for '*Upvaas*' where 'Up' means near and 'vaas' means to live. It is seen that all our major activities tend to take us away from ourselves and do not let you delve within. Eating food is one such activity; it keeps us restricted to the outer world.

The concept of 'fasting', was introduced in India so that a person could get away from these outer attractions and get connected with his inner self. However, very few are able to actually observe fasts in the real sense; others just make a mockery of it. Some people who plan to fast on a particular day overeat on the previous day. The desire to eat is very strong but they resolve to fast merely to fulfil a desire or to please God. The feeling of not getting meals the next day keeps bothering them throughout the day. The imagination of several types of tastes excites the subconscious mind which causes the secretion of digestive juices. Instead of getting in touch with your inner self, your entire focus lies on the food. During the entire day, you tell 50 people that you are on fast. When you repeat it often, you are not happy from within. Your subconscious mind gives result according to this inner feeling and thus, this kind of fast proves to be harmful. On ordinary days, you take your meals and forget about it for the next 7-8 hours but on the day of fast, you dream about food throughout the day, even during the night!

We often lay stress on fruit diet during fasting because fruit is a middle path between the very *taamsik*-natured spicy food, fatty food and the *saatvik*-natured simple plain food. It is also seen that on the days of fasts, extremely heavy diet is consumed in the name of light food such as potato chips, *halwa* (a kind of sweet), *pooris* made of kuttu flour and *sabudana* items, cheese, *lassi*, sweets made of milk products. In such type of fasts, there is neither any feeling of sacrifice nor the tendency to stay away from food for even a short while. There is no dedication towards God nor is there any control on the senses. The only song that keeps playing inside the heart is, **"Babul mora bhojan chhuto jaye"** (O father, I am devoid of my meals). Food! Food!! Food!!! What result will the subconscious mind give in such a situation? Such a fast cannot even please your body, leave aside God. As compared to these, people who take a restricted and controlled diet on routine basis are in a much better position because they have the real feeling of sacrifice and gratitude towards their body.

Those who eat only upon feeling hungry do not have to fast. People who fast are those who oscillate between the two extremes. Once they indulge in uncontrolled eating and then they go the other extreme by choosing to remain hungry throughout the day. They never succeed in coming close to their real self. The subconscious mind, merely through the thoughts, gives complete effect of food to the body. Therefore, if you have a thought about your meals on the day of your fast, then your fast loses its significance. Do not sin against your body in the name of God by pretending to be on fast; it is better to be honest with yourself and eat when you are really hungry.

Hawan (Worship) done by Others Yields no Result

Whenever we worship or pray to God for fulfillment of some need or to get rid of some problem, then as per the law of the subconscious mind, a strong desire or a feeling should build up inside you that you really want to achieve or get rid of something. When you conduct the *hawan* or *puja* yourself, strong and powerful feelings from within are generated and a subtle message is conveyed to the subconscious mind that truly intend to get something out of the *puja* and your in the quest for a path. Since in the absence of the physical act of performing a *hawan* or *puja,* feelings and vibrations are not generated adequately, therefore the performance of these acts is necessary. Based on your feelings and intentions, the subconscious mind generates similar vibrations and transmits them to the Universe, thereby attracting analogous vibrations back from the Universe. However, this is possible only when you perform the *puja,* etc. yourself. Another person such as a *pundit,* priest cannot, by any means, develop feelings and intentions identical to the ones you can generate for yourself. Such desired strong intentions can be generated only by an honest, laborious, selfless and a truly compassionate priest. Such people are hardly present in modern times, who can relate themselves to your problem in the same manner as you. Therefore, whenever, someone else performs the *puja* for us, in 99% cases, we only happen to get some satisfaction and there is only a hope that we would get the desired result. Like this, our life goes on.

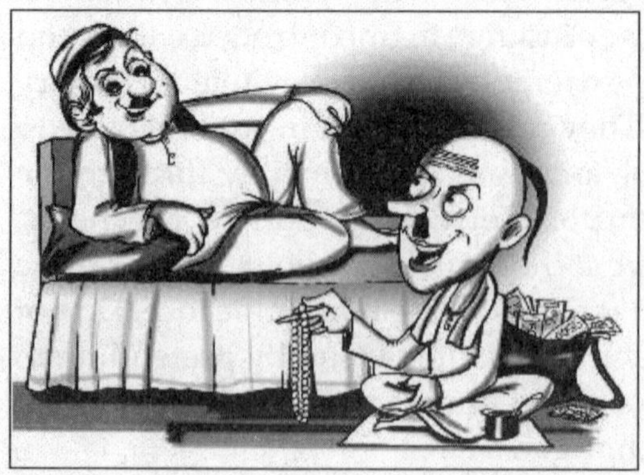

Those people who think that

other person should perform the *puja* on their behalf, unknowingly, convey this message to the subconscious mind that they themselves do not have time and are not much interested or excited about the accomplishment of the task. Therefore, when they hire a *pundit* or a priest for conducting the *puja*, they fail to get the result in 90% cases. The remaining 10% are fulfilled only as a matter of chance or the fruit of their own karma, which they wrongly interpret to be the result of the *pundit's* labour. The fact is that *pundits*, priest etc. earn their livelihood at the cost of our ignorance, fears and blind beliefs. We believe them to be the agents of the God, planets and other supernatural powers. Likewise, the world continues to live in a delusion. It is for you to decide whether you still want to live in this delusion? You decide, whether you have within you the intention which can influence your subconscious in a positive manner.

By having complete faith on God and the infallible laws made by Him, you can generate such positive, powerful and strong feelings to attract anything from the Universe, which no *pundit*, priest or any other person can do for you.

Pilgrimage: If you think that the Gods sitting in the caves, mountains and other big temples are more powerful than the God in your house or if you change the faith in the God and shuttle between different types of gods every second day thinking that the older ones have not helped you, then how do you expect to reap the desired benefit out of your pilgrimage. If you undertake a pilgrimage by

thinking that during your youth, you did not have time and there was not much need for prayers, and that now in the old age, you can please the God by visiting different places of worship and complete the pilgrimage, that by doing so, God will grant you an assured place in the Heaven or help you in your problems or fulfil your desire, then, you are living in a state of fantasy and false imagination. By doing all this, you can never get the benefit of any pilgrimage.

Often people undertake a pilgrimage with a thought that there are a lot of tensions and problems in life; a short pilgrimage will cure all these problems. A pilgrimage may give some relief but it is temporary in nature and as soon as you return back to your normal life, those tensions, problems etc. will resurface in your life. The basic reason of this short-lived effect is that you have faith neither in God nor His indisputable laws. Your method of remedy is only for temporary relief and this fact is absolutely known to the subconscious mind.

If a businessman, in order to get rid of his black money is organising a free pilgrimage for a group of people and you are thinking of joining the group so that you will be able to enjoy the trip for free, then the basic intention inside you is that of free travel which implies greed, miserliness, etc. Your subconscious mind catches the basic intention and thus you will hardly get any benefit from the trip. However, if you can go the pilgrimage on your own with a feeling of devotion and gratitude, the chances of deriving spiritual benefit out of it are much more.

While undertaking a pilgrimage, mostly your internal feelings are of **selfishness** (your basic purpose is fulfillment of your desires), **greed** (to get peace, moksha, prosperity), **sycophancy** (God is quite egoist and needs to pleased), **fear** (not taking God's name may make Him angry and He may give you troubles, spoil your business, etc.), **superficial sacrifice** (there is no devotion from inside, but it is a kind of compulsion otherwise Gods may crate obstacles and problems for you). However, owing to such negative emotions the subconscious mind does not give the desired result.

The purpose of going on a pilgrimage is to visit a religious place and create a positive energy for yourself and connect to your inner being. It is a fact that a spiritually sensitive person can only feel the flow of positive and strong energies at such places. Such places can be a source of immense peace, bliss leading to mental and spiritual upliftment. Life is a stream with two extreme ends – one consisting of tension, excitement and anxiety while the other comprising peace, bliss and upliftment. And, pilgrimage means crossing over from one end of tension and anxiety to reach the other end of love, peace and bliss. Pilgrimage is a shock, an alarm to bring out a person from the state of unconsciousness to pure consciousness. However, for most of the people this change after the pilgrimage is temporary and within a short span of time, they resume to their normal life like before. It serves as a mere splash of cold water which breaks their slumber for a short while and thereafter they return to their old state of slumber. Pilgrimage signifies a holy dip in the Ganges which washes away our age-old ego, desires, ambitions and distortions of life and leaves us pure, pristine and transformed. However, a customary dip in the Ganges, which mostly people take, without realizing the significance of such dip, results in nothing. Any number of such dips, taken without comprehending their true purpose, will only create more illusions in life.

It is now time to wake up, to become conscious and

to delve within. Outer pilgrimages are nothing but a way to escape from the inner, the real pilgrimage. That explains the fact that despite innumerable such pilgrimages, man is still spiritually ignorant. It is merely an illusion of the human mind that a pilgrimage, a dip in the Ganges, a little charity, or superficial service in a temple will wash away all past sinful activities and thoughts and will ensure a good place in heaven.

It is not that these pilgrimages are of no significance at all. In fact, such religious trips serve as initial rungs of the ladder of spiritual upliftment. The ultimate objective is to taking a dip in the Ganges flowing within and to cross over to the other end of the stream of life. The final aim of life is not to visit a place of pilgrimage but to transform oneself into one such place.

Our fears and our beliefs,
***disappoint or inspire us*!**

□

Why do Indian Players Fail in Olympic Games

It has been proved time and again that despite all odds such as poverty, physical handicap, adverse circumstances, people with strong will, determination and conviction have succeeded in achieving the probably impossible goals in their life. Poverty and handicap were neither on their mind nor caused any hindrance.

It is quite disheartening to note that despite immense ability, talent, qualities and hard work, Indian players have not been able to perform to the best of their abilities like the players of other countries. We remain satisfied with a couple of medals and after an analysis for 4 days, things get back to normal, but they do not take pains to find remedy to the problem. The main reason for their failure can be attributed to the subconscious mind.

Every player, somewhere in his mind, has a feeling that foreign players have better facilities, more efficient coaches, higher salaries, etc. This has created an inferiority complex in them. Further, foreigners speaking fluent English are also a cause of their complex. Their better looks, better physiques, fair complexion and financially stronger position are some more factors which adversely affect the psyche of Indian players. The politics in Indian sports and partisan behaviour of coaches and selectors add fuel to fire. The result is that they say – 'I will try to win', which actually implies that they do not have confidence on themselves and are doubtful of their success.

On one hand we try to inspire and motivate our conscious mind through various types of positive suggestions, but our subconscious mind continues to be plagued with negative emotions like dissatisfaction, complexes, grudge, favouritism, politics, fear, greed and ego which adversely affect the subconscious mind. There are laws for success and failures too. It is a law of the Nature that any person who has an aim in his life and tries with utmost devotion, passion and focus to achieve his goal, and who does not get bogged down by the adversities, hindrances and obstacles of life, who toils day and night to reach his goal and one who falls but never fails to rise again shall find what he aims for! No power in the Universe can stop him from achieving his objective. We must always remember that **our success and failure, victory and defeat, hope and despair, poverty and prosperity, joy and sorrow, good and bad, contentment and dissatisfaction are all determined by the subconscious mind depending upon the kind of thoughts and emotions generated by our conscious mind.** Therefore, everything finds its root in the subconscious mind. It is a fact that our Indian players are regularly counseled by psychologists and psychotherapists, but the real knowledge about the subconscious mind should also be provided to them. It is a pity that neither the government nor coaches or the Sports-bodies pay attention to this fact. This is the main reason why the Indian players do not succeed in the Olympics and other international sports events.

In other countries, suggestions on the **'Mind Power'**, of the subconscious mind are invited from the best specialists in the field and the players are freed from their negative fears and emotions. This leads to a better performance which is quite evident in their games. There is an urgent need for training of the subconscious mind in India too.

□

26

Dreams – Shadows of the Subconscious Mind

Dreams are of two types: One, which appear on their own without your having any control over them. In this the subconscious mind is more active. Second, which you create yourself and where the conscious mind has a bigger role to play. Here, we will discuss the former.

It is a view of almost all scientists in the world that we all see dreams. The number of dreams is the least in the state of deep slumber which lasts for not more than 2-3 hours out of an average sleep of 8 hours. This is called the Delta state. During this time, our inner mind is so peaceful that it is unable to see anything. As we come out of this state, our inner mind starts becoming active and it begins to watch the scenes created by our subconscious mind. During the state of sleep, our subtle body comes out of the physical body and starts travelling in the Universe. Mostly we stroll around in the world of the thoughts created on our own. Sometimes, however, we come out of our routine world and then we see unrelated dreams.

Are dreams true? Do they have any implicit meaning or do they carry any message for the future? Yes! Dreams are one of strong media of guidance by way of intuition. We often get answers to many of our complex problems through dreams. Artists, scientists, researchers, often get the requisite guidance and answers to their problems in dreams. However, such guiding and intuitive dreams are rare. Some dreams merely reflect our tension, anxiety and unfulfilled desires whose lasting impressions are formed on our subconscious mind. We are also guided and cautioned by the Gods, Goddesses and ancestors on whom we have absolute faith. Mostly the Gods and Goddesses are those whose image is etched in your subconscious mind. Therefore, Christians and Muslims never see Hindu Gods and Goddesses in their dreams and vice versa.

Indigestion is a Major Cause of Dreams

From my studies and researches, I have concluded that only 10% dreams are inspired by intuition or are likely to give solutions. However, 90% dreams are worthless. Such dreams are common among people who suffer from indigestion, gas, constipation and take a lot of acid forming foods (meat, grain, pulses, egg, cheese, high proteins, alcohol, tea, coffee etc.). When acid in blood gets mixed with gas in stomach, it excites the brain cells and the nervous system. This causes the brain cells to bring out the thoughts suppressed in the subconscious mind and combining these with some thoughts of the outside world, it creates worthless and dreadful vision which we witness in the form of dreams. Therefore, the more acid formation takes place in the body, the more fearful and horrid dreams appear during sleep. If you analyze these dreams, you will find that very few appear logical; most of them are meaningless and devoid of any guiding or intuitive factor. As you control your diet by reducing the acidic intake (high protein, grain, pulses, cheese, eggs) and increasing the intake of basic foods (fruit, salad, juice, sprouts) the acidity level in the blood reduces. As a result, the brain cells and the nervous system do not get excited causing dreams to stop appearing during sleep.

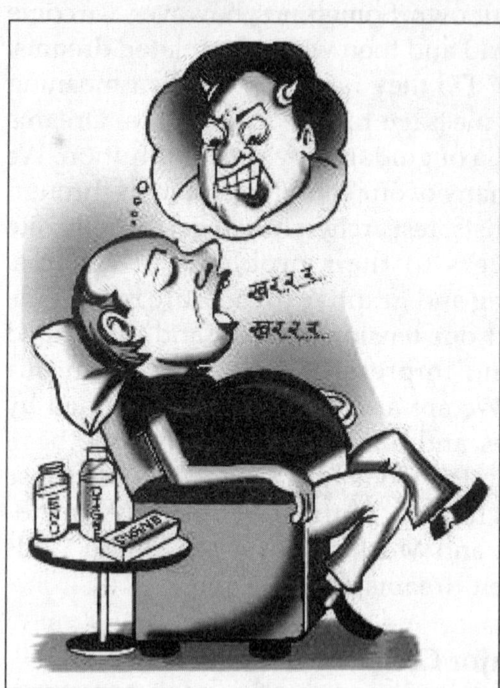

I and my family are living on raw food, fruit, salad, and sprouts for the past 30 years. We use very little grain or pulses in our diet. We eat only when we are hungry; it ensures that food is 100% digested and that there is no question of it getting rot in side the stomach. We consume only one type of solid food at a time; it lets the body digest the food completely and efficiently. It keeps the body free from indigestion, gas and acidity. It keeps the body so light that the presence of stomach is hardly felt. This also helps in getting a deep sound sleep and when we get up in the morning, the body feels fully fresh and rejuvenated. Just before waking up, a few dreams appear that too, seldom. There could a possibility that we see some dreams during the night also, but the sleep is so sound and deep that they are not retained in the memory till morning. The few dreams that appear are also a result of our daily thoughts which activate the subconscious mind to some extent.

My experience on this account is that if we instill consciousness in our daily life and learn to live in the present moment, the barrier between the conscious and the subconscious mind breaks due to which evil thoughts or tension or ego do not reside within and thus the subconscious mind remains free of such thoughts. Therefore, no image or reflection is formed in the form of dreams. The more we drift from the present and indulge in the past or worries of the future, the more turmoil it causes in the thought pattern and the more dreams are seen. **Dreams are the fruit of the sees of the thoughts generated by us. Lesser thoughts mean lesser dreams and vice-versa.**

It is also a fact that if we spend much time in gossip, chat, lectures, sermons and are able to speak our heart out to someone, then the dreams also reduce substantially. However, if these thoughts remain suppressed, then dreams assume an enormous proportion.

The best way to get rid of unwanted dreams is to eat when hungry, take light meals, keep stomach light, meditate and learnt to live in the present. Positive thoughts bring positive dreams and negative thoughts, tension, worries cause negative dreams. **There are reasons behind dreams; when reasons disappear, so do the dreams!**

□

Ghosts are Creations of the Subconscious Mind

Whether ghosts exist or not, is a topic of discussion, but ghosts have been living ever since in the imagination of people. If children are not frightened by taking names of ghosts and spirits and they are not told ghost stories in their childhood, they will never feel afraid to go in the dark or in a frightening environment. Nobody has actually seen a ghost, but we all talk about them and there is a horrible image we have built in our minds about the existence of ghosts. The more we discuss them, the deeper impact it makes on our subconscious mind. Horror films and stories have all the more strengthened this fear. There are no ghosts or spirits in dark and lonely places, but owing to the fact that we grow up listening to such stories and incidents and also the ghostly images created in films and movies, our subconscious mind carves a frightening image as soon as we enter into a dark place. To make matters worse, the shadows formed in the dark give us an impression of the presence of a ghostly figure nearby. We then claim to have seen a ghost. The way we visualize a particular shape or design in mosaic tiles or clouds etc., a similar impression is formed when we see shadows and reflections in the dark.

However, the fact is that ghosts and spirits are merely the reflections of the fears and beliefs etched on our subconscious mind; they have no real existence.

Every cemetery has a watchman who lives there with his family. His children play there all day. On talking to a few watchmen living in various cemeteries, we came to know that they have never seen any spirit or ghost in their entire lives, their children live fearlessly in that area. It is simply because these children have been brought up without the fear of ghosts and spirits in their mind, their subconscious minds do not have any frightful impression and hence, they never see any ghostly images or reflections.

Ghosts are the creations of human imagination. The more deeply we think about these things, the more lasting impact they have on our psyche. Thereafter, they appear before us in the form of reflections, images and even dreams. When we hear someone's experiences then we also begin to imagine about ghosts thereby creating similar impression on the subconscious mind. Thereafter, when we come across lonely and dark places, the ghostly impressions etched on the subconscious mind begin to show and we feel frightened.

Numerous saints, ascetics, *tantriks*, hunters, soldiers, detectives, robbers, dacoits, tribesmen live in forests, caves and other dark and lonely places but none has ever reported to have seen any ghost or spirit. Dacoits and robbers are known to have spent their entire life in dense and wild forests. However, no dacoit has narrated any incident of having seen any ghost.

In horror films, several types of sounds like crackling sound of a door opening slowly, sounds of frogs, lizards, crickets, owls, sounds of crumbling leaves, tip-toeing of shoes, water dripping slowly and sounds of heavy breathing are added to give horror effects to the movie. However, while watching the movie, these sounds get registered in our subconscious mind. When we are alone or sitting in the dark, these sounds start playing in our ears and the subconscious mind instantly connects itself to the past experience of watching the movie. The subconscious mind treats all this as a real scene which in turn, increases our heartbeat and sends a fearful shiver the spine.

By repeating a thought – positive or negative – we accordingly strengthen or weaken the aura and thus experience either gain or loss. As our Gods, Goddesses, Gurus and enlightened souls are merely imaginary entities, so are ghosts and spirits. There is no definite form of god. He is omnipresent but people of different religions and sects worship different forms of gods depending on their convictions and beliefs. These are all gimmicks of the subconscious mind.

Another interesting phenomenon is that Hindus see Hindu Gods, but these are not seen by Muslims. Likewise, an Indian will see ghosts, spirits and divine souls in Indian forms and dresses, while people of China or Japan or Africa see souls and spirits specific to their own countries. This again proves that both Gods and ghosts are created by the images and thoughts imparted to us and engraved on the subconscious mind in our early childhood.

The negative thoughts that we repeat get transformed into layers and shapes of black smoke around our aura and these shapes get converted into horrid faces and become visible to us in our dreams. Therefore, these negative forms and shapes are also the creations of our own subconscious mind.

Why Mostly Women become a Victim of Ghosts and Spirits?

It is seen that world over, as compared to men, women are more prone to become victims of ghosts and spirits. Do ghosts and spirits really victimize women easily and if so, what is the reason?

Studies and researches have shown that the above statement is false and that there is no real presence of ghosts and spirits in women. In fact, women are mostly victims of atrocities and violence in almost all parts of the world. Their desires, views and expressions remain suppressed owing to a male-dominated make-up of the society. Man-made rules but has managed to keep himself free from these rules. He treats woman like a toy for his pleasure, like a machine for household work. He roams around as per his wish and keeps the woman tied up at home like animals. This causes frustration and depression inside the woman and her personality, her qualities and talents are not allowed to develop. This depression and suppression often leads to a situation known as hysteria where her thoughts and expressions explode. This explosion of thoughts and behaviour is incoherent and is therefore construed as 'possession' – which means that she is considered to be under the control of a ghost or spirit.

Instead of getting the woman treated for her psychological and behavioural problem, people of her house seek help from *pundits, tantriks* etc. It is quite unfortunate that even in today's modern times, people go to astrologers and *tantriks* to seek remedies for their problems. These *tantriks* and *pundits* use people's ignorance to their own advantage because it is the only source of their livelihood. Then through their pseudo-spiritual talks and such activities, make people believe that the woman they have brought to him is surely under the possession of a ghost or spirit. This gimmick has been going on for hundreds of years and is still in practice. Since women are more prone to atrocities in India, especially in rural and remote areas, so the cases of ghosts and spirits are also more common in these areas.

Instances of ghosts are very few in cities and developed towns because women have greatly progressed; they are more educated, liberated and aware of their rights. Even today, women are subject to exploitation and violence to some extent but it has considerably reduced over a period of time. However, cases of ghosts and spirits continue to be seen in families where women are still a suppressed lot and have not been allowed to explore and develop themselves.

It is a well-known fact that as the level of education among women has grown, scientific outlook broadened and the number of psychologists, hypnotherapists, healers and spiritual mentors increased, the cases of ghosts and spirits among women has rapidly declined. Developed and educated countries report the least number of ghost cases.

I wish to clarify that there may be some truth in the existence of ghosts but here I am focusing only on the relation between the subconscious mind and ghosts. I visited several countries such as America, Australia and Switzerland, etc. and got to see **'Haunted Houses'**, in these places. However, at no place did I come across incidents of ghosts terrorizing women. The basic reason behind it is education and awareness among women about these issues.

Who is Mostly Affected by Ghosts?

People who are sensitive and emotional are tend to be affected by ghostly feelings more than those who are mentally strong and less sensitive to situations. People with weak nervous system and mental stability are also more likely to be influenced by ghosts. Then there are people guilty of an offence and fearful by nature also get influenced by such things. Ghosts and spirits are negative forces which have a greater impact on people with weak auras owing to some illness, grief, depression, anxiety etc. Actually, 'possession', by ghosts and spirits are technically known as psychic attacks or psychosomatic disorders which can be easily treated by healing the root cause, correct lifestyle, right eating habits etc.

In the end, I would also like to mention that 10% people really suffer from psychic attacks and effects of ghosts and spirits, but in order to cure these problems they should not seek help of *pundits* and *tantriks*. Instead, taking help of energy specialists and Reiki healers is sure and rapid way of doing so. The reason is that in a country like India, only 5% *pundits* and *tantriks* are genuinely knowledgeable, the remaining 95% are fraud and mislead innocent people. It is a myth that negative energies and psychic attacks cannot be removed; in fact even an illiterate simple person is capable of doing it provided he is a Reiki channel. Negative energy, in any amount, remains only in the aura. It is very easy for a Reiki channel to clean the aura and the *chakras* (energy centers in the body). He also knows how to provide a protective energy shield around the body. People who are mentally weak and sensitive by nature, have a weak aura and thus the ghosts, spirits and other souls –evil and divine – are visible to them in the form of smoke. Such people are called Clairvoyant.

Regular practice of meditation, Reiki, *sadhna*, etc. causes the nervous system and the inner being to resonate with divine energy and such bodies also become sensitive to vibrations. Some people are born with this ability; it is because of the effect of past lives where they have been working with energy and their bodies and minds have evolved to that level during those past lives.

Here, the most important thing to understand is that these spirits and souls around us cannot communicate with us. They can see, hear and feel the situations around and can even approach us if invoked, but they cannot establish contact with us. Their presence can make the surrounding light and enjoyable or heavy and irritable depending upon the kind of soul they are. It is possible to establish contact with these souls only at the subtle level, not at the physical level. The method of going to the subtle level is either through meditation or in sleep. During the deep state of meditation, the physical body becomes relaxed and then the subtle body rises to enter into the subtle world. It is in this world, that the spirits and souls of our ancestors, Gurus, etc. meet us and either guide positively or frighten

us. These souls are actually the source of intuition. Since they cannot correspond directly, they choose the method of intuition to either inspire to do or dissuade us from doing something. Simple and good people are surrounded by helpful and divine souls while people who are evil and negative by nature never get any guidance or intuitive help from such souls.

□

Poverty and Prosperity are Gifts of Subconscious Mind

Who makes us rich? Who makes us poor? Is it God or destiny or any other power? No, it is neither God, nor destiny or any other force. It is your own subconscious mind that makes you rich or poor. Let us try and understand this.

It has been often repeated in this book that God has no control over this activities of this world or your life or movement of stars and planets. He has simply made the rules of the game and it is these rules which govern everything in this Universe. By making use of these rules, anyone can become rich or ignore these rules to become poor; God has no role to play in it. The choice is ours and the result of this choice appears in the shape of our destiny. A child is born in a particular family – rich or poor – in accordance with his past life *karmas* (actions). Therefore, it is not the decision of God. Whatever thoughts, behaviour patterns and habits your subconscious mind has imbibed from you during the course of your past lives, finally determine your fate in the present life. Likewise, the thoughts and habits in your present life will be recorded by the subconscious mind and it will eventually determine your fate in future life.

If you are able to bring awareness into your life and free yourself from the bondage of old habits and karmas and you are able to set up a new mindset, develop new thoughts and build up new energy, then you automatically come out of the old patterns and start moving towards a better and brighter future. It is a simple game where one takes a minor decision and chooses to enjoy the shade rather than get burnt in the sun. You may, out of greed, ego or stubbornness choose to remain in the sun but then it is your choice; God has no role to play in it. Therefore, each moment, we create our present and future through our conscious decisions and choices. **You must remember that nobody is interested in making you rich or poor.** We all want to become rich but each day, we program our subconscious mind though unknowingly, by focusing more on the limitations and thus, we attract more and more poverty in our lives.

We put the boat of our desire to become rich in the ocean of prosperity and also push it painstakingly in the hope of reaching our destination some day. However, we spend the entire life merely trying to reach our goal, but never achieve it because your boat remains anchored to the shore with chains of age-old beliefs, orthodox thoughts, misconceptions, *karmas* of the past lives, etc. Thus your entire life passes while simply staring towards the Island of prosperity. In the end, when we do not reach our goal, we only strengthen the following statements:

- I will get it if it is there in my destiny.
- What is to be shall be.
- I need blessings of God.
- I will not get it before time and more than my destiny.
- Time, circumstances, friends, relatives are not worthy enough; they did not cooperate with me.
- I believe in simple living and high thinking; money is not important for me.
- Money is root cause of all evil.
- Everybody does not have the same fate, etc.

If we are poor today, it is because of the subconscious mind and if rich, the credit again goes to the subconscious mind. In order to progress in life, we have to get rid of the old belief systems. Therefore, to prosper and become rich, we have to recognize the negative emotions and come out from these. It is also important to understand the laws of prosperity and adopt them. **Absolute prosperity and richness have indisputable laws. The manner in which anyone can use things like TV, Computer, etc. with ease, similarly by adopting the laws of prosperity, a common man can attain unprecedented heights of prosperity.**

Our childhood, environment, family, parents, relatives, friends, educations, teachers, etc. determine our mindset. If you are living in a poor family, your mindset has the following thoughts:

- Money does not grow on trees; it also does not drop down from the sky.
- One has to toil really hard to earn money; it is not easy to earn.
- We are poor and unfortunate by birth; God is less kind to us.
- One should learn to live within his limits.

- Luxurious and comfort-oriented lifestyle is extravagance, sin and crime.
- Others barely live hand to mouth; how do we earn money and why should we live in luxury.
- Satisfaction is supreme; it is best to live within your resources.
- Do not increase your desires and needs.
- People like us cannot attain great heights.
- Our parents did not give us the facilities; our friends betrayed us.
- We do not cross our limits; we do not dream.
- Money and prosperity is the root cause of tension.
- People, who earn money, do so dishonestly; we work like labourers to earn money.
- We do not run after money; money is not very important for us.
- God is giving us meals; less expectation implies less sorrow.
- Foolish people pursue luxurious life.
- What shall we do with so much money; it will not go with us at the time of death.
- Simple living, high thinking; we have not earned money, but respect.

Many such thoughts and concepts may seem to be quite virtuous and upright, but in fact they are the "Best laws to remain poor" and are the most infallible methods to avoid riches and prosperity. These thoughts are main causes of the destruction of India because they have formed the basis of our underdeveloped ideology. We claim to have supreme spiritual powers which can turn around the entire world. But where are these powers? Where are the saints and sages and mystic people who make such claims? If this ideology continues to govern our mindset and actions, then it will take hundreds of years for Indians to become rich and prosperous.

The above mindset is etched deeply in our psyche. It is important to get rid of these thoughts because these are the 'anchors', the shackles for your progress which will never let your ship of prosperity to sail successfully. It is now time to break these shackles and make ourselves free from this bondage. All this is possible only by following the Laws of the Nature. **God is not kind and benevolent on those who earn money; in fact such people are benevolent to themselves. They are able to break the shackles of their narrow mindedness and dare to think big and see bigger dreams. God is not partisan of the West, who gives immense wealth to America, Europe and other western nations or bestows them with more technological development or is less kind to India, Asia or such other nations.**

The kind of negative or positive feedback that you give to your mind determines your entire life and your lifestyle. Our life is the outcome of these thoughts and beliefs.

The laws of becoming rich and wealthy are very simple–

1. Understand and recognize the right kind of concepts and theories about wealth and come out of the limitations. Realise that you can earn as much wealth as you desire.
2. Every individual has a unique quality. Learnt to realise your potential and your goal of life. Make endeavours in the field which you are comfortable in. This will save a lot of labour and hard work and give you success more easily and quickly.

Lord Krishna tells in the Gita that you must live and follow your own nature; never follow or live the nature of others. It is also said – **'The crow tries to walk like the swan, and forgets his own gait.'**

Mostly, parents want their children to follow the routine professions such as doctor, engineer etc. or want them to take over the family profession or business. Fulfilling social obligations or getting them settled in good families after marriage etc. are their favourite goals. They even persuade their children to find government jobs so that their future is secured.

Contrary to the above theory, if we tell our children that God has made you. So recognize your talent and potential and pursue it with passion. Anything you do, do it with excellence. Be the best in your field. If we impose our dreams and aspirations on you, we will destroy your life with our own hands. Live your own nature, fulfil your dreams and never copy anyone. Get inspired by great people, but have your own fragrance. However, today most of the parents want to convert a rose flower into a lotus or wish to make see oranges growing on an apple tree.

3. In this world, people are always looking for honest, hard working experts in their fields. Be one and success will find you one day!
4. Dream and aspire. Shun satisfaction. Create new and innovative things. Find new paths.
5. Prosperity does not trickle from the sky. You have to use your talent, your dreams and aspirations and your firm belief system to attract prosperity from the Universe with the help of your subconscious mind. Once we succeed in converting ourselves into a powerful magnet, then everything we need comes to us through the laws of attraction. Is it not unfortunate that most of the world's wealth is confined to merely 2% people of this earth?

Is it not a matter of inspiration that most of the successful and prosperous people such as Bill Gates, Ambani, Ford, Lakshmi Mittal have all risen from modest families. If you are able to understand the Laws of Nature and the science of subconscious mind, no power in this Universe can stop you from becoming prosperous.

More than anyone, God has been kind to us,
He is willing to give to the one who is ready to take.

If there are rules of poverty, there are also rules for prosperity. You become whatever kind of rule you pursue. Terms such as destiny, coincidence, miracle, God's will etc. are used by people who is ignorant, lazy, weak and timid.

□

Role of Subconscious Mind in Absolute Surrender

There are only two ways of reaching the spiritual zenith – **resolution** and **surrender**. Resolution is the part of mind, science, analysis and logic whereas surrender is the path of emotion, faith, and absolute trust. The path of resolution was followed by Buddha, Mahavir, Krishna, Nanak, Patanjali etc. The path of surrender was pursued by Mira, Chaitanya etc. Conscious mind and ego are more active in the case of resolution and this ego accompanies a person till he reaches the zenith. Gradually starting from the physical form and reducing to the subtle form, a person reaches the top till the residue of self and ego is also shed. Resolution requires ample labour at each step. If the task is not completed in this life, one may be required to take another birth; the contribution of subconscious mind is quite limited in this method. Subconscious mind is influenced by the conscious mind, its faith and resolution and creates only those types of vibrations and brings the person into motion. The path of resolution can even create an illusion and get stuck midway.

However, contrary to the above, the method of surrender is free from these obstacles. A person moving on this path does not get stuck with analysis, logic etc. and thrives fully on absolute faith. The path of surrender is however not as smooth as it appears. People on this path also have illusions that they have completely surrendered to the will of God but when they are faced with serious problems on the course of life such as diseases, crisis,

loss, death etc., and they feel afraid or worried, it only reveals how weak and superficial their surrender is. It is seen to be limited to conscious level only and does appear to have seeped down to the subconscious level. And thus we instantly return to our initial state where the hurdles of life shatter the mirror of our self-created illusions. The real pursuers of the path of surrender do not have scope for analyzing grief, joy, life, death etc. They do not have the ego left to be worried, tensed or feel anxious. They have completely surrendered to the will of God. What is left is only the subconscious mind. As soon as we develop this feeling of surrender, our conscious mind takes a back seat. Subconscious mind generates the thought that 'I' has vanished and what is left is only 'He'. The entire programming received by the subconscious mind converts the personality of the person completely. He neither gets disturbed, worried nor tensed, when faced with a trouble. This helps in attaining the state of joy and bliss. The subconscious mind tries to protect us by attracting positive waves in the aura. These feelings are deeply ingrained in the aura. For such people bowls of poison is converted into nectar, scorching heat into cool and chill into the warmth of mother's lap.

The more one dedicates one's actions to God and Universe, the more one's subconscious mind generates positive and favourable results because there are no obstacles of fear, ego, greed and evil intentions to hinder one's path. Therefore, the subconscious mind can only comprehend the feelings of surrender and positive attitude which causes only favourable outcomes for the people following this path.

As the walkers on the path of resolution move forward the existence of the subconscious mind tapers down. For the pursuer of the resolution path, the distinction of the conscious mind vanishes and what remains is the element of self which merely witnesses. Neither the subconscious mind of such people develops nor do they form any habit or personality. There is no emotional suppression, no duality. Owing to a nature devoid of any reaction, no new *samskaras* develop in. The more a person lives in the state of unconsciousness, the more the subconscious mind expands, habits become strong and reactions takes place on their own. As the gap between the conscious and the subconscious widens, we tend to lose control over both of them. Contrary to this, as the conscious and the subconscious come close, the necessity of meditation (resolution-surrender), also increases because there is only one way to control or weaken the conscious and the subconscious – meditation. Meditation breaks the wall between the conscious and the subconscious and what remains is, **'pure consciousness'**.

□

30

All Symbols Work because of the Subconscious Mind

Human mind, instead of long sermons and lectures, is more quickly affected by symbols. Therefore, all significant thoughts, powers and statements have been expressed in symbolic forms. These symbols have worked equally well from the ancient to the modern civilizations. Both Science and religion make use of symbols. One is able to identify a company or a brand merely by seeing its symbol. However, here, I will not discuss the symbols of countries, companies or brands, but the symbols used in the *yantra, mantra* and *tantra*.

How do symbols affect us?

There are two main objectives of making a symbol – either we represent different types of energies of the Universe in the form of small symbols or we choose symbols to express our own thoughts. For example, in India we make the symbol of

swastika and write '*shubh laabh*' (fortune and profit) with it.

When someone introduced you to *swastika* for the first time, he must have described it to be a symbol of purity, God and good fortune. And you accepted it. Now, whenever, you see *swastika,* you instantly get a feeling of purity, Godliness and good fortune. It proves that symbols affect the subconscious mind. If you do not bring your logic or analytical mind in-between, the feelings connected with that symbol are instantly produced. Therefore, it can be said that symbols condition the subconscious mind and are capable of recreating the same effect again and again. This helps in building up the related energy within us as soon as we see these symbols. You have also been told that the symbol of Red Cross (which forms a part of the *swastika* symbol) means 'Doctor'. Now when you see the Red Cross sign, it does not generate within you the feeling of purity or good fortune, but that of doctor! The sight of *swastika* develops purity, and the intention instantly changes to that of doctor the sight of a Red Cross.

If you see the flag of India, you get feeling of India; the American flag will cause you to think about America. *Swastika* may be one of the most powerful and mystical symbols in the world, but it will fail to create the feeling of respect or divinity in a Muslim or a foreigner because for them, there is no faith or thought attached to it. The more faith, belief and devotion we have towards a symbol, the more powerful and positive energy it builds up. Since a *swastika* fails to create any energy for the Muslims or Christians etc., we can conclude that the basis of the origin and creation of energy is our faith and acceptance.

In India, Tibet and many other places, there is a practice of worshipping various kinds of Gods, Goddesses and creating varied kinds of yantras and abstract amulets. It is worth-mentioning that none of these charms and amulets have any power. The power is actually created with our own energy through our acceptance and faith.

Yantra – Yantra is a geometrical shape or a design through which by using a special picture or lines, we express the force of powers and energies of the Nature and those of our own thoughts. All these pictures, lines or symbol are called Yantra.

In India, all the symbols, designs, geometrical shapes, statues of Gods and Goddesses come under the category of 'Yantra'. We also make '*Swastik*' sign, also called '*manglik*' (fortunate) in which a '+' (plus) sign is made and four clockwise lines are joined to it.

Then we write our feeling on its sides – '*shubh*' (fortune) and '*laabh*' (profit). It means that may fortune and profit keep getting added up in our house from all the directions and make us move always in forward and future-oriented direction (depicted by the four clockwise lines). Now, how does this *Swastik* proves to be beneficial? It surely benefits us if we put our feelings and thoughts into it powerfully while writing. *Swastik* is just a means to express our feelings and thoughts. It is actually our feelings that give strength to it otherwise, *Swastik* by itself does not have any power in it. Since thoughts create vibrations, weak thoughts create weak vibrations and strong thoughts create strong vibrations. If *Swastik* alone could bestow fortune and wealth, the wholesaler in whose godowns, there are innumerable

Swastik lying would have been the richest man in the world. Likewise, a small hawker sitting on the pavement selling *Swastik* would also have been wealthy and fortunate.

Yantra (symbols) actually help us to make our thoughts strong and powerful. An intention of wealth and fortune with *Swastik* surely yields better results as compared to the same intention without *Swastik*. Therefore, we need a symbol to empower our thoughts and intentions. Any symbol that once goes deep inside our subconscious mind immediately produces feelings associated with the symbol. According to this programming of the mind, *Swastik* implies a "Pure and sacred symbol of beneficial energy," whenever you would see *Swastik* anywhere your feelings would automatically, become pure and sacred. Now remove the four clockwise lines from this *Swastik*, thereby leaving just a plus (+) sign. Now when you look at it, your feelings would again change and you would start thinking about doctor/hospital because your mind has been programmed to understand that a plus sign in red colour means a doctor/hospital. As such, symbols have a tremendous importance because symbols form the language of our subconscious mind. That's why so many symbols have been formed till now. Now, if you show this *Swastik* to the Germans, they would look at you with hatred because a cruel and violent German dictator, Hitler had used reverse form of *Swastik* as his symbol. It only implies that no symbol has its own power. It is the thought that gets generated on seeing that symbol which gives it the requisite power – negative or positive. No other religion, except the Hindu religion, has got any importance for *Swastik*. In other countries, *Swastik* is merely a good design and not a fortunate or sacred symbol.

We should remember that all the symbols, Yantra, Gods-Goddesses in the world have been formed by different thoughts of different people. A man-made symbol cannot be more powerful than man himself. Though we create symbols, Gods-Goddesses and Yantra for our convenience but gradually, become their blind slaves. We need symbols, Gods-Goddesses and Yantra because they are the only means of creating forceful thoughts but simultaneously, we should be aware of the scientific viewpoint behind them and should not follow them blindly.

All our Gods-Goddesses represent various types of Natural energies. People across the world and of other religions have a question that why are there so many kinds of Gods-Goddesses in the Hindu religion? If we worship one God each daily, his/her turn would perhaps come only after 2-3 months. Is it madness or some intricate science? There is no doubt in the fact that the depth with which the scholars of India have studied the secrets of the Universe or the Nature, no other place in the world has done it. All Gods-Goddesses represent different energies because we have classified every God into a form of energy and created symbols for it. There are hundreds of energies in the world so there are hundreds of Gods-Goddesses too. Fire is an energy so we have Fire God (*agni devta*), for wind, we have Wind God (*vayu devta*), for clouds we have Rain God (*Indra devta*), for money, there is Wealth Goddess (Lakshmi devi), for knowledge, there is Goddess of Wisdom (Saraswati devi). We also made a symbolic statue of all of them so that by seeing them, their associated feelings would arise within us. Other Gods like

Brahma, Vishnu, Mahesh, Durga, Ganesh, Indra, Lakshmi, Saraswati, Kali (Chamundi), Bhairav etc. do not actually exist in human form. All these are merely symbols and they are also essential so that they should generate associated feelings and thoughts within us when we see them. They have all now become an integral part of our psychology.

Lord Shiva is pure form of Universal power. When the serpentine *kundalini* power (*Shakti*) hisses upwards through the *chakras*, the third eye of the person opens up and he experiences eternal peace and tranquillity. Tranquillity is represented by the Moon and stream of water. The ox standing next to Him there symbolizes sex, which He has won over and raised upwards. Shiva can be a part of every body because everyone has got this ability but our scriptures and scholars have added strange stories and concepts to it which give an impression that some supreme power named Shankar was indeed born but he has been hiding somewhere in the sky.

Till the time, humans would keep taking birth on this earth, Lord Shankar will also exist because He is an integral part of the human form. No human means, no Shankar.

Shiva-Shakti is actually not a male-female personality. A union of two opposite but complimentary energies is what we call Shiva-Shakti. In China, this is called 'Yin-Yang' energies. These are actually positive-negative energies. Since the entire Nature is governed by these two energies, the balanced form of these energies is called Ardhanarishwara. These two energies are working inside every person. Therefore, every person, by balancing these two energies can become 'Ardhanarishwara'. Goddess Durga, represents the unlimited power of woman. Therefore, Durga has several hands, which represent several forms of energies. Durga rides the Lion which is the fiercest animal. This symbolizes that Durga has controlled the fiercest form of energy and likewise, man can also control energy and use it for his benefit. Since 'power', is feminine, these powers have been depicted as Durga. The Black and the White Bhairav symbolize negative and positive *tantrik* powers respectively. The Black Kali (Chamundi) represents negative powers, which stand over the kind 'Shiva', depicting the negative power. The garland of human skulls, beheaded skull, hanging tongue, black body etc. show the negative feelings of this power and this symbolic form of Goddess is used by *tantriks* for their worship and meditation.

Likewise, all our Gods and Goddesses have been created to represent different forms of powers (energies). You cannot pray for wisdom by keeping Lakshmi's photo in front, you cannot invoke fire god by keeping wind God's photo in front because it is the law of nature that the kind of thoughts we have inside us, similar vibrations are created in the Universe and the similar type of vibrations come back to us. This is the Nature's law of Attraction–Repulsion. This is a self-governing law. Nobody controls it. Therefore, the scholars of India, in order to invoke different forms of energies, to generate different types of vibrations, have created different types of images and symbols. All these symbols are actually Yantras.

'Shri Yantra', is also a geometrical design comprising 108 triangles. A triangle is a symbol of upward movement (growth and prosperity) with a strong foundation. These triangles are on all the four sides representing multi-dimensional growth and prosperity. Shri Yantra is constructed like the Mount Meru showing prosperity at each step. No energy gets built up by nearly keeping the Shri Yantra in your house unless you create positive vibrations with a sincere heart and strong emotions. These vibrations then, become 'Mantra'. Mantra is not a miraculous thing. It is just a subtle science of attraction and repulsion of vibrations, about which I will explain later.

In books, there are hundreds of Yantra like Kali Yantra, Kuber Yantra, Narayan Yantra etc. or tables and strange designs with numbers written in them. We sometimes, think them to be possessing magical powers. But it is not so. So, never think like this. For example, *Swastik*, Red Cross, these

above-mentioned designs are also ordinary geometrical symbols to express a specific type of feeling. This is also necessary because man has several types of desires and emotions. However, *tantriks*, astrologers, *pundits* etc. exaggerate their importance. It is nothing but nearly a part of their profession and a means to frighten a person and force him to believe it. Never believe these Yantras. You can make your own Yantra and fulfil your goal/desire. Ancient people developed these symbols according to their needs. If you have the power of creative visualization, you can design and prepare better Yantras than these. *(The technique to design you own Yantra is taught in the Reiki Grand Master Course).*

Since we have been deprived of such topics which should, otherwise, be a part of our preliminary education, we believe these ancient Yantras to be magical and miraculous. We are so influenced by the term 'ancient' that we presume that such potential is not possible today. In the name of being 'ancient', we are willing to blindly accept and worship any thing rubbish that is offered to us. You may not believe it but our human potential is much more advanced as compared to the ancient times. We can create better things today provided we are able to get rid of the ghost of 'ancient' that always haunts us. It does not mean that all the Yantra of ancient times are fake or wrong. These are several designs and Yantras which are indeed wonderful but you must never think that you cannot worship or pray without them.

Those who had earlier prepared these Yantras were also new creators. Most of the Yantra do not express the power of energy within them. They have just been made for the sake of it and we have been blindly following them since then. This trend may continue and the future generations may also follow them blindly. This is how blind faith carries on its journey. Our basic aim is to unveil these secrets so that every person should become wise, a scientist and become aware of these things.

The simple principle that works behinds these charms and yantras and amulets is as to how much faith and conviction these are accepted with. The more faith we develop in the, the more powerful they become and vice versa. This is why the blind followers find these charms and amulets more effective and worthy because the logic and reasoning of the conscious mind does not prove to be a hindrance in its working. Therefore, the more incoherent and complex these yantras (which can't be easily comprehended or analysis by logic), the better they function. If try to comprehend or analyse the shapes and meanings of their designs, they will begin to lose their sanctity and effectiveness. One who is completely devoid of doubts and apprehensions as regards the effect of these yantras and amulets derives the maximum benefit from them.

The science of symbol is based on the law that all secrets should be not be revealed. Some should remain unsolved because the human nature is such that as soon as the needle of suspicion comes into motion, it instantly and firstly, punctures the wheel of faith. Had there been no subconscious mind, these symbols and signs would have been of no use at all.

It is for the above-mentioned reasons that the mantras and yantras are intentionally made incoherent and absurd. If you are given a mantras as simple as '*mangal bhavatu*', (wish your welfare) there would be absolutely no impact on your mind. However, if you are told a mantra such as, "*tili tili tum tum, gili gili bum bum*" (which actually means nothing), you will neither understand it nor doubt it. And thus it will create an unquestionable faith in your mind leading to the development of extremely powerful energy. However, there is the other side to this as well. Such practices also cause a great damage to the spirit of science and tends to encourage blind faith, dogma etc. in the society. It makes a person handicapped, weak and dependent and he is never able to realise the enormous and unlimited potential hidden inside him. Upon taking help of the crutches of such mantras, he fails to stand on his own feet. The kind of conditioning of your mind ultimately determines the amount of strength or weakness in your life.

Your own fears, your own beliefs,
Give you hopes or cause despair.

□

31

Subconscious Mind Turns Impossible into Possible

All the seemingly improbable tasks have been accomplished only with the power of the subconscious mind. Whether it was the dream to fly an airplane or to step on the moon, whether it was about constructing an amazing building or an adventurous activity, it is the subconscious mind that has made it possible. These tasks are impossible for the conscious mind to accomplish because the conscious mind has limitations; it reaches a certain level and then refuses to go and think beyond. Contrary to this, the subconscious mind has unlimited potential and is connected to unrestrained energy sources of the Universe. It can attract these energies with the help of intuition, clairvoyance, spiritual guidance etc. We can see that whatever dreams man is seeing now, he is able to fulfil and realise them. All the amazing achievements of Science are the outcomes of the power of the subconscious mind. Just as we cannot induce sleep into the eyes forcibly, we cannot create music, art or invention using the conscious mind. However, as soon as we let the conscious mind relax and take a back seat, the subconscious mind becomes active and sleep befalls upon us and all the intuitive thoughts, ideas and guidance also begin to take form. Be it science, art, music or literature, the subconscious mind has proved its merit invariably in all aspects of life.

Conscious mind is based on logic, reasoning and analysis while the subconscious mind is based on faith and imagination. One who dares to dream and has a conviction strong enough to make that dream come true, is rewarded by the supreme powers of this Universe which help him to achieve his goal and fulfil his dreams and desires. Man will continue to see dreams and strive to make such dreams come true. It is with this power of the subconscious mind that man has been able to reach the heights of material world, attain financial achievements and succeed in miraculous scientific endeavours.

The subconscious mind is fully capable in accomplishing impossible tasks. It is the conscious mind which is weak and which creates limits and restrictions for us. It fails to go beyond its boundaries, fails to see new dreams and hence fails to prosper. Those who dared to think big, dream big and resolved to reach their goals were called crazy and crackpots in the beginning, but these crazy and crackpots are the people who have succeeded in changing the world and made it develop and prosper. It is a fact that even the best possible man shuns from doing the improbable tasks because his conscious mind becomes the biggest barrier.

How are impossible things achieved: Suppose, you want to lift a man of 100-150 kilograms with just two fingers. Whatever method you apply or howsoever confidence you fill up in your conscious mind, you will not be able to even move that person. Now you take the help of your imagination and feel that the power of your worshipped God or Goddess is flowing in your body and your strength is gradually increasing. Consequent to your imagination, when you open your eyes and try you will be able to lift the person easily without feeling his enormous weight. Actually what happens during this process is that your subconscious

A Still from popular TV Show 'Mano Ya Na Mano' Dr. N.K. Sharma and Mr. Anand Sharma Lifting a 100 kg women just by two fingures without feeling any weight.

mind treats your imagination as true and you hardly feel the weight of the person. However, having return to consciousness, if you try again you will not be able to lift or move him. As soon as we free ourselves from the state of consciousness and take help of our faith, belief and imagination, we are able to accomplish impossible tasks. Likewise, people walk barefoot on embers or pierce their tongues and bodies with needles without any pain because the subconscious mind treats the imagination as real.

You can bend a hard Steel Spoon within few seconds by suggesting your subconscious Mind. (One can learn this Magic in our Mind Power Workshop)

Under the same law you can bend a stainless steel hard spoon like a rubber effortlessly in a few seconds which could have otherwise required a lot of force to do so. A task which you are unable to do with your conscious mind despite your full power and best efforts, can be done almost effortlessly using the power of your subconscious mind. It also shows that we make extreme efforts to accomplish certain things in our life and during the process, take tension, feel stressed out and worried. However, if we use imagination and belief and put this power of the subconscious mind to proper use, the same goal can be achieved without much effort and stress.

We have demonstrated and proved the truth behind these laws thousands of times in our Reiki workshops. It is a matter of great misfortune that mostly people are unaware of this inherent power of the mind and neither these techniques are taught in the schools and colleges. As a result, we are forced to live in boundaries and remain satisfied with very little achievements in our life whereas the fact is that every person can attain great heights of success and prosperity in his life.

In a Rajasthani village named Badi Sadri of the Chittorgarh area, all ladies of the village have to prove their fidelity and purity by taking out 10 *pooris* each with barehands from the vessels containing boiling oil. It is surprising that all the ladies accomplish this feat easily because their subconscious mind feels that since they are loyal and pure their hands will not get burnt. This powerful and emotional thought is accepted by the subconscious mind and it gets materialized. If they would think that their hand will get burnt, it would surely happen. It is not benevolence of God but the power of their subconscious mind which protects their hands and makes things happen strictly as per their belief.

In the same way, the people who walk barefoot on embers are also made to believe that if they chant a mantra or take deep breaths or think of target across the bed of embers, their feet will not get charred. And they follow the instructions meticulously without having an iota of doubt in their minds and hence, succeed in walking on the embers without getting burnt. By keeping your focus on a mantra or your breaths etc. takes the attention of the conscious mind which prevents the negative or damaging thoughts to come to your mind. This principle is often used by people without being aware of it. For example, labourers while moving a very heavy object make strange sounds. This actually helps them together to rise above their consciousness and accomplish the task. Similarly people going on pilgrimages while moving on difficult stretches also make sounds and chant loudly to overcome the barriers of conscious mind. Behind all this, works the law of the subconscious mind which makes one free of the limitations of the conscious mind and helps to achieve impossible goals.

Think! Imagine! Dream and Believe;
And achieve with a little effort; so simple is
The principle of the subconscious mind!

One can walk on Fire without any burns, through the power of Subconscious Mind.

□

Subconscious Mind Creates Your Lines of Destiny

Every human takes birth according to the *karmas* (actions) of his past life and brings along with him the lines of destiny reflected on his palms. These lines on your palms are created by your own actions in the past life. They never change. However, when you imagine new things, see new dreams develop new goals and desires and create strong intentions and feelings from your subconscious mind, it leads to a pressure on the underdeveloped cells and nervous system of the body causing new lines to appear on the corresponding areas of your palms. Through powerful imagination and strong emotions, we can bring new and positive changes in the palm lines. New thoughts can be made to strengthen the new lines so much that it can weaken the effect of the old lines. Programming of the subconscious mind can create

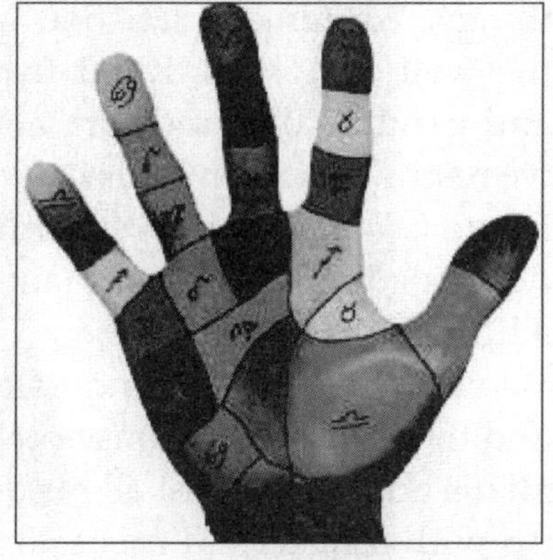

new lines and cause to raise new mounts on the hands. Our present hand is the result of the past actions; similarly, the actions of the present moment can remake the hand of our future. The kind of action (seed) determines the kind of result (tree) we will have in the future. It is not incorrect to say that your hands represent the accurate state of your subconscious mind.

Your hands show the outline of the *samskaras* around you. Your hand represents your entire state of mind. It also gives complete and accurate information about your qualities, nature etc. Your horoscope may not give the exact account of your destiny but the hands do not tell a lie. The only thing required is that the person who studies the lines should be an expert.

We have forgotten to ask

The fact is that we have almost forgotten to ask for things. We remain satisfied by seeking little favours from the well of wishes. Right from our childhood, our casual and genuine demands are also refused and suppressed or we restrain our demands on our own. Our teachers, parents, friends, mentors etc. either cut the wings of our dreams and desires advising us to remain grounded or they allow only a little flight to us.

The person who understands the rules of the Universe and those of the subconscious mind is capable of achieving all his goals and fulfil all his dreams. We have been brought up with a restricted mentality due to which we feel afraid and embarrassed to think big or see bigger dreams.

Just once, imagine that God is willing to give you a boon and is asking your wish. In such a situation, you should be ready with your wish-list even if it is absurd or unrealistic. You must know what to ask if God wants you to grant you three wishes! You should not hesitate to ask a thing of the highest order. Once you should write your three demands on a piece of paper, you will realize how small your wishes are!

Universe is an ocean of unlimited wealth. We have spent our lives filling our spoons and bowls from this ocean of wealth. There are only a few people who have dared to pump out huge amounts of water from this reservoir. The amount of water that we take depends on our thoughts and intentions.

Why should we not live in the most palatial houses and enjoy the most wonderful luxuries of this world? The truth is that we are not at all serious about enjoying the best things of the world. We tend to call those fortunate who enjoy these luxuries and continue to remain in the underprivileged lot. Therefore unless the thought is there, there will be no discovery, no desire to achieve. So think, dream and send the powerful thoughts of your intentions in the Universe so as to attract wealth, health and prosperity in your life. To dream is not sin. Do not attach it with guilt or greed or fear. Such thoughts corrupt the desires and vitiate our dreams. Play your role and learn to ask for yourself and for the world and prove that you are indeed the son of God!

You are the Biggest Shani!

Planets and humans are the creations of the same God and each one has to continue to tread on the path of life through expression of one's nature. Planets move on their axis and man on his. The movement of planets has no connection with progress or retreat of man's destiny and neither they have been created by God for this purpose. Numerous tribes on earth are even today living a disease-free life. The people of these tribes live for more than 100 years, but does it mean that *shani* (Saturn) or *mangal* (Mars) are kinder to them in any way? The answer is No! It is surprising that the ill-effects of *shani* are mostly proclaimed in India which forms only 2% of the world's area; there is no mention of *shani* in the remaining 98% of the world. There is no such concept as *rahu, ketu, kaal sarpyog, maanglik kanya,* etc. There is no doubt that the more a Nation is ignorant, uneducated and orthodox and believes in *tantriks* and astrologers, the more fearful it will be of *shani*.

In fact, you are the biggest *shani*. The *shani* inside you has many faces like ignorance, blind beliefs, fears, negative emotions, ego, skimpy dreams and limited desires. The real *shani* may trouble you for a maximum of seven-and-half years and cause some damage as well, but the *shani* of your misconceptions and ignorance trouble you not in just this life but in the lives beyond. Knowledge and enlightenment frees man from the imaginary bondage of these planets and makes them appear God-like, revered and oceans of love!

Ignorance is the greatest Shani !
For enlightened person there are only
laws of Health, Wealth and Happiness.

□

Infallible Law of Attraction

A Definite Way to Achieve Dreams, Desires and Goals

The Laws of Nature are infallible! It is the greatest irony that Nature has given us such a wonderful and miraculous Law of Attraction to attract anything we desire from the Universe but due to our faulty thought process, we ourselves have become the biggest obstacles in our path to success, abundance and bliss. We, at Reiki Healing Foundation (RHF), have used the secrets of this Law to attain what we desire. Let's vow to shatter the chains of misery and misfortune and use this wonderful Law of Attraction to achieve our dreams, desires and goals!

—Dr. N.K. Sharma

The Science of Attraction: The science of attraction is an exact science, like algebra or arithmetic. There are certain laws which govern the process of attraction. Once a person learns and obeys these laws, he will attract anything with mathematical certainty.

You Are A Living Magnet: The Law of Attraction says that you are a "living magnet" and that you invariably attract into your life people, ideas, opportunities and circumstances as per your thoughts. Nature treats everyone alike. Whatever seed you plant, nature will grow it. Whatever thought-seeds you plant in mind, nature will grow as well. It is entirely up to you. When you change your thinking, you change your life. Nature is always true, serious and severe. It is always right, and the errors and faults are always those of man. Only to the apt, the pure and the true does She resigns herself to and reveals her secret. The Secret of Attraction is: I attract to my life whatever I give my attention, energy and focus to, whether positive or negative.

By reading this article you'll come to understand why and how this happens.

Like Attracts Like: You are the most powerful magnet in the Universe! What most people don't understand is that a thought has a frequency. We can measure a thought. And so, if you are thinking that thought imagining in your mind having that you need, building that company, finding your soulmate ... if you're imagining what that looks like, you're emitting that frequency on a consistent basis. Your thoughts emit the magnetic signals that draw the parallel results back to you. "The predominant thought or the mental attitude is the magnet, and the law is that like attracts like, consequently, the mental attitude will invariably attract such conditions as correspond to its nature". Thoughts are magnetic, and thoughts have a frequency. As you think, those thoughts are sent out into the Universe, and they magnetically attract all like things that are on the same frequency. Everything sent out returns to the source. And that source is you.

Universal Laws Are Exact: We live in a Universe in which there are laws, just as there is a law of gravity. The law of a attraction is also a law of nature. It is precise, and exact. Nothing can come into your life, unless you charge it through persistent thoughts. Most of us attract by default. We just think that we don't have any control over it. Our thoughts and feelings are on autopilot, and so everything is brought to us by default. Researchers tell us that we have about 60,000 thoughts a day. Our feelings let us know, what we are thinking.

Focus Raises Energy: To increase your vibration means to give your desire more positive attention, energy and focus. The Law of Attraction brings more of whatever you give your attention, energy and focus to. If, however, you identify your desire and don't give it attention, energy and focus, then there is no manifestation.

What you Resist Sticks to you Like Glue: Any time your thoughts are flowing, the law of attraction is working. The law works continuously. It's an ongoing process. What you are thinking now is creating your future life. You create your life with your thoughts. Since you always think, you always create. What you think about the most, appears in your life. Your thoughts are seeds, and the harvest will depend on the seeds you plant. If you are complaining, the law of attraction will bring more situations for you to complain about. The law is simply reflecting and giving back to you exactly what you are focusing on with your thoughts. You can completely change every circumstance and event in your entire life, by changing the way you think. You know vibration means your mood of feeling. So whatever you see/observe the same you feel and whatever you feel creates the power of attracting the same.

Feeling is Important – Not the Word: Each time you read your affirmation, you'll have a reaction based upon how the words make you feel. Law Attraction responds to the vibrations you send out based on how you feel, not based on specific words you use. If, for example, you tell yourself that you have a happy, slender body when you do not, or when having a happy, slender body feels unattainable you'll create negative vibrations. You'll send out a vibration of doubt (a negative vibration), which the Law of Attraction will respond to by giving you more of the same, even though it's unwanted. A positive affirmation can have a negative vibration. Most affirmations don't work because the Law of Attraction doesn't respond to words, "It responds to how you feel about the words," you use.

Size is Nothing to the Universe: It is not difficult to attract something that we consider huge. The Universe does everything with zero effort. The grass grows effortlessly. It's all about what's going on in your mind. It's about what we say, "This is big; it's going to take some time." And, "This is small; I'll give it an hour." Those are our rules that we define. There are no rules for the Universe. You provide the feelings of having it now, it will respond to whatever it is. There is no time or size for the Universe. It is as easy to manifest one dollar as it is to manifest one million dollars. The process is the same, but the reason why one may come faster and the other may take longer is because you thought that a million dollars was a lot of money and that one dollar was not very much!

A Picture is Worth a Thousand Words: You can also make a dream book by cutting out pictures of all of your goals and pasting them into the book. Make sure to go

through your dream book at least once a day. The result can be nothing less than miraculous! The Law of Attraction does not care whether you are remembering, pretending, playing, creating, complaining or worrying. It simply responds to your vibration and sends you more of the same!

How Do I Know If I'm Doing It Right: After you've written your Desire Statement, go back and read it. Next, ask yourself how do you feel does your Desire Statement make you feel great? If not, then revise your statement so that you feel better on reading it. Remember, the Desire Statement is meant to raise your vibration and to help you include your new desire in your vibrational Bubble. Having strong desire and a strong doubt cancel each other out.

Having a Strong Desire Is Not Enough: It is only when your resistance is removed that your desire is manifested. The faster your resistance/doubt is removed, the faster your desire can be realized. It takes no time for the Universe to manifest what you want. Any time delay you experience is due to your delay in getting to the place of believing, knowing, and feeling that you already have it. When you are on that frequency, then what you want will appear.

Your thoughts are Made up of Words: Your thoughts and your feelings create your life. It will always be that way. Guaranteed! There are no exclusions to the law of attraction.

If something came to you, you drew it, with prolonged thought. When we can begin to open ourselves up to that, the ramifications are awesome. It means that – whatever thought has done in your life, it can be undone through a shift in your awareness. You have the power to change anything because you are the one who chooses your thoughts and you are the one who feels your feelings.

To take Einstein's intention even further, you can affirm and proclaim, ***"This is a magnificent Universe. The Universe is bringing all good things to me. The Universe is conspiring for me in all things. The Universe is supporting me in everything I do. The Universe meets all my needs immediately."*** Know that this is a friendly Universe! Begin right now to shout to the Universe, ***"Life is so easy! Life is so good! All good things come to me!"***

All good things are your birthright! You are the creator of you, and the Law of Attraction is your magnificent tool to create whatever you want in your life. Welcome to the magic of life, and the magnificence of you!

Many of us don't Know what to Ask for: We do not know what we really want or how to ask. Most of us are out of touch with our real needs and desires because we were continually ignored, rejected or ashamed of expressing them as a child. So it became safer and less painful not to. We simply buried our desires. The second barrier to asking for what we want are the limiting and negative beliefs that have been programmed into our subconscious and which now silently control all of our actions. Where do these beliefs come from? We are born with an empty data bank that has to be programmed. Many of us are hindered in our asking for and getting what we want by the negative and limiting beliefs, we have taken on from our parents, teachers, religious places and the media. We settle for less and we sit in judgment of others who are getting what we want.

Search for your Dreams and Write them Down: As many as you can before you ask for something, you have to know what it is that you want and you have to believe it is possible to get it. Your feelings tell you very quickly what you're thinking. Think about when your feelings suddenly took a dive-maybe when you heard some bad news. That feeling in your stomach or solar plexus was immediate signal for you to know what you are thinking.

That thought magnetically attaches itself to the like frequency, and then within seconds sends the reading of that frequency back to you through your feelings. Put another way, your feelings are communication back to you from the Universe, telling you what frequency you are currently on. Your feelings are your frequency feedback mechanism! When you are feeling good feelings, it is communication back from the Universe saying, "You are thinking good thoughts." The next time you are feeling bad or feeling any negative emotion, listen to the signal you're receiving from the Universe. In that moment you are blocking your own good from coming to you because you are on a negative frequency. Change your thoughts and think about something good, and when the good feelings start to come you will know it was because you shifted yourself on to a new frequency, and the Universe has confirmed it with better feelings.

You are a human transmission tower more powerful than any television tower created on earth. Your transmission creates your life and it creates the world. The frequency you transmit reaches beyond cities, countries and the world. It reverberates throughout the entire Universe. And you are transmitting that frequency with your thoughts! The pictures you receive from the transmission of your thoughts are the pictures of your life! If you want to change anything in your life, change the channel and change the frequency by changing your thoughts.

□□□

Unlock Miraculous Powers of Your Body, Mind & Soul

(Two Greatest Powers of the Universe can manifest all impossible dreams)

In a 2 Day Life Transforming Workshop

With World Renowned Grand Masters Dr. N. K. Sharma & Dr. Savita Sharma

An Unparallel Course

First of its kind in the world

Transformed millions

World Class

Scientific

Myth Breaking

STORMING INDIA & ABROAD

Unbelievable Benefits

1. You will learn greatest eye opening secrets of all time.
2. You will unleash your own inherent, hidden psychic & mind powers.
3. You will free yourself permanently from age old blind beliefs, superstitions, ignorance, fears of future, black magic, accidents, all negative forces and effect of planets.
4. You will be able to heal yourself, others, plants, animals & environment. Liberating yourself from incurable diseases, sufferings & past karma.
5. You will be able to create your own destiny, future & circumstances.
6. You will learn the simplest secrets of unlimited wealth, superb health & self realization.

Highlights of the Dynamic Course

REIKI - The Art of Touch 'n' Heal

The Science of Aura

The Science of Chakra

Telepathy - Distance Healing

Power of Intention

Power of Intuition
- The Sixth Sense

Clairvoyance - Seeing invisible

The Third Eye(Inner Vision)

The Power of Subconscious Mind

The Science of getting rich

Law of Attraction
(To manifest Dreams, Goals & Desires)

The Law of Permanent Cure & Nutrition

Remedial Exercises

Mental Cleansing – Healing Body, Mind & Emotions - A Re-Birth experience

Self realization - Towards Enlightenment

Excel in Education/Career/business /profession

The law of Harmonious Relationships

Lots of Fun-Laughter-Music- Dance & Meditation!!

How Long Do You Want To Continue To Suffer From...

Diseases, Bad Relationships, Poverty, Ignorance & Failures ?

Dr. N. K. Sharma's
Other Eye Opening Books

Para Psychology and Spirituality

1. The Miraculous Power of Sub Conscious Mind (Eng.)
2. Adhyatamik Paakhand (Hindi)
3. Guru Dhunden Beech Bazar (Hindi)
4. Dhyan Beech Bazar (Hindi)
5. Mahatma Rogi Kyon? (Hindi)
6. Ishwar Ke Naam Par Dhandhli (Hindi)

On Health and Nutrition

1. Milk – A Silent Killer (Eng.)
2. Wonders of Natural Diet (Eng.)
3. Good Bye To Indigestion (Food Combination) (Eng.)
4. Prakritik Aahar Ke Chamatkar (Hindi)
5. Sahi Pakayen Rog Bhagayen (Hindi)
6. Swadisth Prakritik Vyanjan (Hindi)
7. Rogkarak Doodh (Hindi)
8. Anaaz Rog Karak Hai (Hindi)

Available at:
Reiki Healing Foundation (Trust)
56-A/ED Block, Madhuban Chowk,
Pitampura, Delhi-110 034
Ph.: 09811179047. 9911331113, 011-27311456
Email: info@rhftrust.com
Website: reikihealingfoundation.net

Reiki Healing Foundation
A fight against all Blind Beliefs and
Realisation of the all hidden
Powers of Mind

Dr. Nand Kishore Sharma's
A Revolutionary Research Book

MILK
A Silent
Killer

Unfolding Startling facts about 'Animal Milk' Based on Scientific and common sense approach bringing A GREAT REVOLUTION IN NUTRITION

The author explains:

- Why Animal milk is not fit for human consumption?
- How does it affects silently and kill?
- How it initiates disease like. Cancer, Asthma, Allergy, Heart Disease, Cold and Cough, Constipation, Amoebic Dysentry, Gas, Colitis, Severe Digestive Impairments and Many More Diseases.

You too may be a Milk Victim
Exciting and eye opening chapters

- Milk and its relation to childhood sufferings.
- We do not need any milk substitutes
- Curd-No relation to longevity and health
- Hazardous effects of high (Animal) Proteins
- The best source of natural, right non-toxic Proteins and Calcium
- Proper food combination and safe use of milk
- Milk – A Cancer initiator
- Milk Fats and Coronaries

- Milk Calcium is dangerous
- The protein myth
- Pasteurized milk – A dead food
- Ice Cream or poisoning
- Un-natural milk production
- Milk-Borne Diseases
- The definite way to increase mother's milk
- The dangerous contamination in milk etc. and many more

Also find an answer to Natural Diet of Man for Optimum Health – Rejuvenation and Longevity

Price Rs. 195.00 (Postage Extra)

Translated in Several Foreign Languages
(A Life Positive Publication)

Where The Entire Search For Mysteries and Secrets Ends

Join World's Pioneer Institute of Psychic Studies

REIKI HEALING FOUNDATION

(ISO 9001:2008 Certified)

(Internationally Awarded For Quality, Service and Mission)

FOR WORLD CLASS COURSES

- **Reiki and Mind Power** – Explore all your healing and Mind Powers from 1st Level to Grand Master Level.
- **Past Life Therapy** – Become a professional past life therapist to resolve all Karmic Issues.
- **Dowsing** – A Pendulum quarries system Search, Choose and Heal.
- **Crystal Ball Gazing** – Develop your natural intuition powers and inner visions to see and sense Past, Present and Future.
- **Third Eye Activation** ***(for Kids and Adults)*** – See and Sense everything Blindfolded by developing your hidden Psychic Senses for extraordinary Brain Power and Achievements.
- **Clinical Hypnotherapy** – Become a professional Hypnotherapist to re-programme subconscious in every field of life.

Contact for further detailed information:
REIKI HEALING FOUNDATION
40-A, ED Block, Madhuban Chowk,
Pitampura, Delhi -110 034
Ph.: 9911331113, 9990771116
Email: info@rhftrust.com
www.reikihealingfoundation.net

Reiki Healing Foundation's Activities

HEALING TEMPLE - A last hope for incurable and chronic problems (***Where the entire search for Health and cure ends).*** **Heal everything** – A holistic wellness centre for regular Reiki sessions, Past-life sessions, Personal hypnosis sessions, Aura scanning, Counseling and consultation for all health, financial, relationship, mental, emotional, psychic, educational and spiritual related problems.

DISTANCE HEALING – One of the world's Largest Distance Healing Group. RHF is probably one and only largest centre in the world where highest number of successful distance healing is done for all health and other life related problems. RHF's unparallel distance healing has saved thousands of sick people's life, business, relationship and other global problems.

AURA SCANNING – A latest advanced digital technology to scan invinsible subtle energy of the body (AURA) to know present and future potential diseases, vital force, healing effects, chakra status etc.

It also scans various negative and positive energies of objects and vastu of building, offices and houses.

FREE MASS REIKI TRAINING – RHF is the one and only Reiki organization in the world which is passionately spreading Reiki to the general masses by organizing Free Reiki Courses all over India and abroad. Enlightening every individual with their hidden body, mind and soul power leading them to disease free long life, natural vegetarian (Vegan), life style, financial freedom and self realization. Thus saving the whole humanity and ecology.

PUBLICATIONS - RHF has published several eye opening and revolutionary articles, books, audio and video clips. It also distributes a popular monthly magazine by the name of 'Wonders of Reiki' free of cost to its channels across the world since the past 20 years.

FINGER TALE – Know your exact Mind Blue-Print for which you are design for. A unique and scientifically proven finger prints analysis to know your original talent for 100% Success.

Contact for further detailed information:-
HEALING TEMPLE
56-A, ED Block, Madhuban Chowk, Pitampura, Delhi - 110 034
Ph.: 011-27311456 (M) 9560 54 3434
Email: healingtemple@rhftrust.com
www.reikihealingfoundation.net

डॉ. एन. के. शर्मा

मेरा लेख एवं मेरी कविताएँ ही मेरा सच्चा परिचय है।

इशारे पे मत लटक, स्वयं के गुरू को जान।
दूसरों के पंख क्या काम के, अपने पंख पहचान॥

यूँ तो जन्म हजार लिए, एक और जन्म लिया तो क्या?
जिस दिन जागा तभी जन्मा मैं, अंधा बनकर जिया तो क्या?

हमसे ज्यादा ईश्वर ने हमारा किया विचार है।
खूब लुटाने बैठा, वो लूट लो जो तैयार है।।

तुमसे बड़ा अजूबा है क्या कोई जहाँ में।
तुमसे है ये दुनिया, वरना क्या रखा जहाँ में।।
खुद से भी आगे क्यों तुम भगवान ढूंढते हो।
सब कुछ मिला हुआ है, क्या तुम खोजते हो।।

खुदा से कह दो जन्नत से मिटा दे मेरा नाम।
क्योंकि धरती पर ही मिल गई मुझे स्वर्ग से बेहतर
अवचेतन मन की शक्तियाँ।।